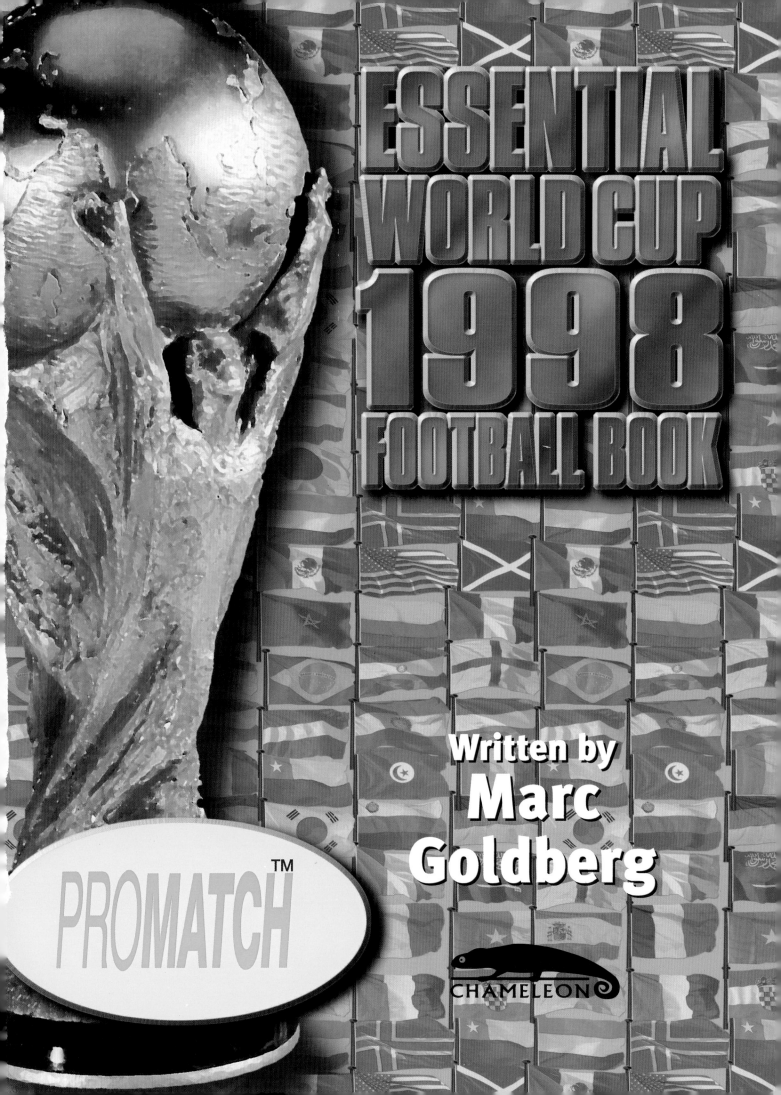

ESSENTIAL WORLD CUP 1998 FOOTBALL BOOK

Written by Marc Goldberg

PROMATCH™

CHAMELEON

First published in Great Britain in 1998 by Andre Deutsch Ltd,
76 Dean Street London W1V 5HA
www.vci.co.uk

Andre Deutsch Ltd is a subsidiary of VCI plc

ISBN 0233 99420 3

Printed and bound in Great Britain by Jarrold Book Printing,Thetford,Norfolk

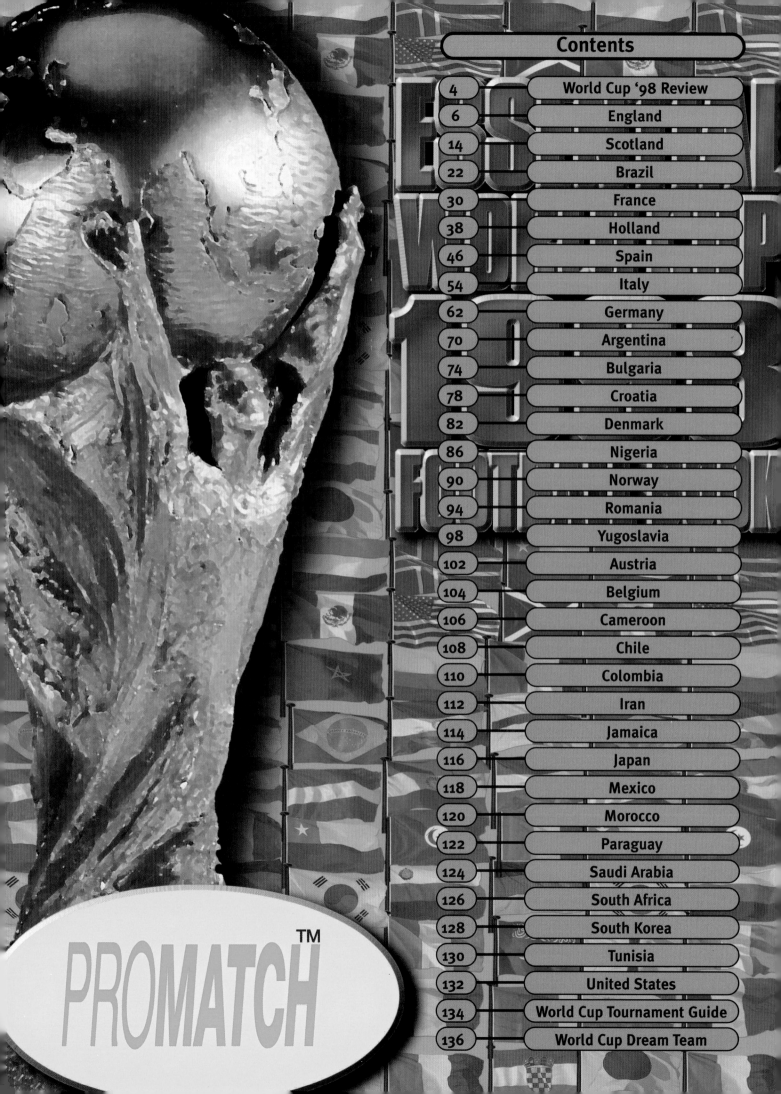

Contents

PROMATCH™

The tension and excitement for France '98 is building. It can be felt around the world, the biggest sporting tournament is getting ever nearer. After the gruelling ordeal of qualification England and Scotland won over the hearts of the United Kingdom by reaching the World Cup.

The British teams have been simply outstanding to have qualified automatically after such difficult qualifying groups but it is the English who will surely have more of an impact in France. Glenn Hoddle has built a squad that has everything; experience, fresh faces, talent, steel and most important of all, a superb team spirit. Though Glenn found that some of his experimental teams did not work he has a firm idea of what he feels is his strongest eleven. The spine of the team is of great importance to the England manager where he sees Seaman, Adams, Ince and Shearer his most influential players. Previous World Cups have seen opposing teams combat our tenacious football and then win us over with superior ability-how times have now changed. Players such as Gascoigne, Beckham, Sheringham and boy wonder Michael Owen can match the Brazilians with flair and skill, but they must be consistent. Hoddle and his team stand a great chance of coming home with the World Cup.

Let's not forget Scotland. Though rated as complete underdogs in their qualifying group Craig Brown steered his team to deserved qualification. When taking over the reins of the Scottish team Craig had very little resources and few quality players to work with, now there is a whole new era in Scottish football. Not only has the Scottish league finally turned into more than just a one horse race but there seems genuine quality within the ranks. With Colin Hendry and Gary McCallister in the team they have two of the most natural born leaders who will be in France. They have always been thought of as the perennial strugglers who lack ideas and a potent strikeforce; Gallacher and Ferguson have the potential to prove the doubters wrong and put Scotland on the footballing globe.

The World Cup is a chance for players around the world to show what they can do in front of billions of viewers. Some crumble under the tense pressure and then there are the players who can be made into a world superstar overnight. There are sure to be players who will undoubtedly have extortionate price tags put on their heads but then there are those who everyone expects to do well.

Favourites Brazil are without doubt believed to be the strongest force who will be in France. Every player is naturally gifted, though some more than others. In Ronaldo and Roberto Carlos they have the two best players in the world and can be unbeatable on their day. With all the dazzling skill and never-ending talent their are also fears within the Brazilian camp that there is a lack of team spirit. Recent results in warm-up friendlys saw a disillusioned Brazilian side put in some extraordinary performances. Comfort for the other teams or simply a facade to cleverly deceive the rest of the world?

Germany and Italy are still unquestionably strong and will be very hard to beat. The Italians have a lot to prove to their fans after failing to reach the World Cup through automatic qualification, unrest in Italy usually causes a serious backlash so be prepared for some fiery performances from Cesare Maldini's team.

Though the atmosphere in the World Cup will be tense there seems to be a buoyancy about the tournament. Teams such as Jamaica and Japan go into their first ever World Cup Finals and will surely be everyone's second favourite team-they will simply just enjoy the occasion.

All the ingredients are there; the stadiums are magnificent the weather should be perfect and the fans are full of optimism-the football is now the crucial element which will bode for what could be the biggest footballing spectacular ever.

What are their chances?

When England did not qualify for the World Cup in 1994 the nation felt the pain of having to watch the biggest soccer tournament in the World take place without their famous country. Now 8 years since their last World Cup appearance they are ready to show what the world missed in USA '94.

Glenn Hoddle has constructed a squad that is being tipped as one of the favourites in France '98. Having taken a team that had been refurbished by former maestro Terry Venables, Hoddle has polished up a squad that is ready to take on the world.

There is a blend of youth and experience, vital to a team that uses the squad system the way England do. In players such as Beckham, Scholes, the Nevilles, Rio Ferdinand and Nicky Butt, there is the youth and drive that give England a cutting edge. But it will not only be the youngsters who will be giving it their all to impress, there are those in the squad for who it will almost certainly be their last international tournament. Seaman, Gascoigne, Ince, Sheringham, Adams and Wright are a select few who will be giving it their all at showing the rest of the world what they can do as they bow out of international duty.

The key lies in the form and the camaraderie the players can generate in the England camp. If the spirit is there then they can win the World Cup. The players will give it their best and will return triumphantly to England with the Jules Rimet trophy under their arms

Group G

Monday June 15
ENGLAND V TUNISIA
Monday June 22
ENGLAND V ROMANIA
Friday June 26
ENGLAND V COLOMBIA

David Beckham

Age	Caps	Value
22	-	£12.5 million

Once branded as one of 'Fergies fledglings' David is now one of the most established midfielders in European football. His skills and ability seem to continue to grow whilst it seems that his feet are still firmly on the ground, not like some Manchester United stars of the past! Since being picked for his first cap in the opening match of the Qualifying rounds he has never lost his place. His pace, agility and especially his ability at set-pieces are now being matched by work-rate and tenacity, making him the all round midfielder. If he can stay free of injury and concentrate on his football then he will play a major part in England World Cup campaign in France.

Sol Campbell

Age	Caps	Value
23	12	£8.5 million

At only 23 years of age Sol is one of the most accomplished defenders on the international scene. Having already passed the '10 cap' barrier he will almost certainly go on to play in the next two World Cups.

Yet in the Premiership his team, Tottenham, did struggle but there was never any doubt about his ability and it was Sol that came to the rescue on many an occasion. With the world not that familiar with Campbell it is in this World Cup that he can make a real name for himself.

Gareth Southgate

Age	Caps	Value
27	22	£4 million

First brought to international stardom under the reign of Terry Venables he has shown that he can still do the business with Glenn Hoddle. After such disappointment in Euro '96, especially for Gareth, he has shown his true fighting qualities and his determination to keep his place in the national side.

At the age of 27, Gareth is in the prime of his career and he shows that when he performs on the pitch. He is quick and dominating in the back and can play in the sweeper role, he will play an important part for England if they are to do well in France.

Graeme Le Saux

Age	Caps	Value
29	21	£4.5 million

Graeme, now 29, is one of the most unlucky players in the squad. Having been talked about so often as being one of the most promising players in the English game, injury has halted his progress on the international scene.

In France, Graeme will finally show the rest of the world what he can do. His nimble feet and quick mind have earned him much praise over the years and following his £5 million move from Blackburn to Chelsea he has been in quite dazzling form.

Paul Gascoigne

Age	Caps	Value
30	54	£4 million

There is not a lot more that can be said about the infamous Paul Gascoigne. When stepping on the world footballing scene in Italy 8 years ago he made as big an impact as anyone had made for their country in years.

Now, two World Cups on, the more mature and experienced Gazza is hoping that he can go one better than Euro '96 and Italy '90. He is still a wizard on the ball and is one of the only England players who can turn a game with a moment of exquisite skill and inspiration.

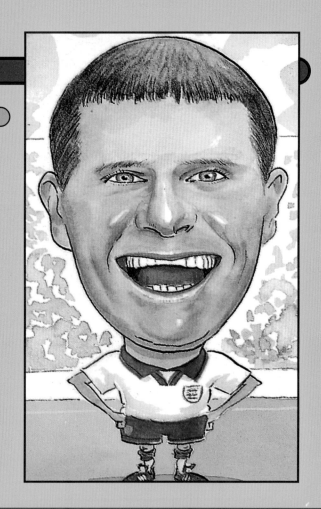

David Batty

Age	Caps	Value
29	26	£4 million

When fans of the English game talk about a player who they would like in their team, David Batty is a name that always comes up. Much of his work does go unnoticed though he plays a vital role in the centre of the midfield.

His 'terrier' like attitude on the pitch has earned much praise, even though he sometimes gets carried away which does lead to trouble. David is a player that puts his heart into the cause and will be putting in all he possibly can to help England succeed in France.

Teddy Sheringham

Age	Caps	Value
31	29	£3.5 million

It will almost certainly be Teddy's first and last World Cup, which will hopefully inspire the Manchester United forward even more to do well in France. The qualifying rounds saw Sheringham and Shearer carry on their electrifying partnership and the whole of England hopes that they will continue after prolonged injuries to both of them.

Though England do not play with a big target man up front Teddy does take up the role of supplying much of the fire power for Alan Shearer.

Tony Adams

Age	Caps	Value
30	47	£4 million

Questions will be asked about the fitness of Tony, but if he can get over his injury problems he will prove to be one of England's most important players. His commitment to the team along with his leadership and determination are vital to England.

The Arsenal stalwart is a quality defender. He displays sheer confidence in his positioning and tackling. He is very rarely tested by the big occasion and that is why he will prove so important to the England defence.

Gary Neville

Age	Caps	Value
22	23	£8 million

At only 22 Gary is still a youngster but is now regarded as an England regular. With over 20 caps under his belt he is more than capable of performing at the highest level.

Alex Ferguson regards him as one of the best defenders in Europe, by watching his performances for both club and country there would be little argument. He is quick, a good passer of the ball and strong in the tackle - an asset to the England squad.

David Seaman

Age	Caps	Value
34	38	£3 million

Though the emergence of Ian Walker and Nigel Martyn has created competition to the England number one there has never been a doubt who will be pulling on the goalkeeper's jersey in the opening game against Tunisia. His heroics in Euro '96 and his quality performances for Arsenal have never really seen his place in jeapardy. At the age of 34 it will almost certainly be his last major international competition and there is no doubt that a player of David's calibre will still be able to show the quick responses and dominating force in the box that he has showed throughout his career.

Steve McManaman

Age	Caps	Value
25	19	£6.5 million

Although he may not figure in the first team, Steve is a player who is a potential match winner. His form for Liverpool in the '97 and '98 campaigns produced moments of pure genius, though on occasion he was still inconsistent.

Glenn Hoddle could use Steve as a natural winger or perhaps more significantly in a free role behind the strikers. Either way Steve has the ability to change a match single handedly. Certainly a player who could make a big impact in the World Cup.

Profiles of the rest of the squad

Nigel Martyn

The Leeds goalkeeper is making a strong claim for the number one spot. He has waited a long time for his chance and will be a more than able replacement if called upon. A fantastic shot-stopper.

Rio Ferdinand

A 19 year-old defender that has the chance to show the rest of the world why he is being tipped as one of the best young defenders since Bobby Moore. His speed and ability to bring the ball out of defence will prove useful to the England squad if called upon.

Gary Pallister

Though the years are not on his side he showed in the 97-98 season that he still has what it takes to play at the highest level. He has one of the coolest heads in the game and will be hoping he gets his chance in surely his last major international tournament.

Philip Neville

Whilst his brother has more of a chance of making the first team, Philip is destined for great things and is being tipped to be an England regular for years. If he does make an appearance in the same side as his brother it will be the first time two brothers have plays alongside each other in a World Cup since the infamous Charltons.

Andy Hinchcliffe

When being recognised as international quality at the beginning of Glenn Hoddle's reign, Andy has come into the side and performed very well either in the centre or left hand side of defence. His free-kicks and corners could provide dangerous ammunition for Shearer and co.

Robert Lee

Another versatile player who has proved in the past that he can come into the national side and reproduce the same form that he can for Newcastle. He will be looking to bow out of international duty with some impressive performances in France.

Nicky Butt

Nicky will seriously look to breaking into the first team in France. After having an outstanding season for Manchester United he is being raved about from all corners of the country. A blend of skill and tenacious tackling makes him an all-round complete midfielder.

Tim Flowers

Though for years he has plays second fiddle to David seaman there has never been any doubting Tim's goal-keeping qualities. His performances for Blackburn in the 97-98 season helped them to a European place and he will hope that he gets his chance to help England progress.

Paul Scholes

Le Tournoi in '97 saw Paul show that he is more than capable of playing at the highest level and he could prove to be England matchwinner. He is the little dynamo in the centre of the midfield that England have lacked over the years and if given his chance he will be hard to move out of the team.

Robbie Fowler

Still only 23 Robbie has much left in him. He has yet to show that he can score the goals at international level, as he has done for Liverpool, but is another that if given his chance could be hard to be replaced.

Andy Cole

Andy's international career seemed as though it was going nowhere until he found himself in sparkling form in the 97-98 season. He has found his shooting boots once again and if in the mood could notch an important goal or two in France.

Ian Wright

The infamous Ian Wright is a legend. His charisma and determination won him a place in the heart of England fans everywhere with his performances in the qualifying rounds. He may not get a first team place but you can be assured that every minute he plays in France he will give his absolute best.

Michael Owen

At the age of only 17 he made his Premiership debut for Liverpool and is now the talk of the country in the build up to the World Cup. His speed is phenomenal and he has the potential and frame of mind to go on to be one of the stars.

ENGLAND

How they got there

Group 2

Date	Home		Away	Score
01-Sep-96	Moldova	vs.	England	0:3
05-Oct-96	Moldova	vs.	Italy	1:3
09-Oct-96	Italy	vs.	Georgia	1:0
09-Oct-96	England	vs.	Poland	2:1
09-Nov-96	Georgia	vs.	England	0:2
10-Nov-96	Poland	vs.	Moldova	2:1
12-Feb-97	England	vs.	Italy	0:1
29-Mar-97	Italy	vs.	Moldova	3:0
02-Apr-97	Poland	vs.	Italy	0:0
30-Apr-97	England	vs.	Georgia	2:0
30-Apr-97	Italy	vs.	Poland	3:0
31-May-97	Poland	vs.	England	0:2
07-Jun-97	Georgia	vs.	Moldova	2:0
14-Jun-97	Poland	vs.	Georgia	4:1
10-Sep-97	England	vs	Moldova	4:0
10-Sep-97	Georgia	vs	Italy	0:0
24-Sep-97	Moldova	vs.	Georgia	0:1
07-Oct-97	Moldova	vs	Poland	0:3
11-Oct-97	Georgia	vs	Poland	3:0
11-Oct-97	Italy	vs	England	0:0

Alan Shearer

Age	Caps	Value
27	35	£15 million

Without any doubt Alan is one of the most vital players to the England squad. Though he suffered much of the 97/98 season through injury he typified his character by recovering months before schedule and returning as though he had never been out of the game.

For the last 4 years he has been the most feared striker in the English game and is thought of as one of the most deadly finishers in the world. It is amazing to think that this is Alan's debut performance in the World Cup finals, though be assured that he will not let the occasion get to him and he will carry on banging in the goals.

FINAL STANDINGS

England	8	6	1	1	15	2	19
Italy	8	5	3	0	11	2	18
Poland	8	3	1	4	10	12	10
Georgia	8	3	1	4	7	9	10
Moldova	8	0	0	8	2	21	0

World Cup Odds

6/1

What are their chances ?

Many believe Scotland are going to France to make up the numbers but the manager, Craig Brown, is spreading the word that his side have exciting times ahead of them. Having qualified through the best runners-up spot, they showed many that they are a side that is beginning to add skill and flair to the discipline and strength that have always featured in Scottish teams.

Brown has done wonders. He came into the international scene four years ago and has since revamped an ageing side that was going stale.

There is genuine hope and excitement among the Scottish fans who believe that they have the players to progress. In Collins, Hopkin and Lambert there is the flair that they have craved, but there is still the grit and strength with players such as Hendry, Boyd, and Calderwood. Not only do they have the blend of vigour and ability, they have a potent forward line in Gallacher in Ferguson. Both are outstanding strikers who could form one of the most exciting partnerships in France.

They do not have the easiest of groups but have shown in the qualifying rounds that they have the ability to overcome sides of the quality of Austria and Sweden.However, in the past the Scots have suffered from questionable temperament and they are infamous for losing to the minnows of international football: we all remember Costa Rica!

Craig Brown and his side open the Championships against Brazil. They have what it takes to get through their group, and the match against Norway will prove most vital. Role on those Braveheart headlines as the Scots get through their group; anything else would be a bonus.

ONE TO WATCH

Group A

Wednesday June 10
SCOTLAND V BRAZIL
Tuesday June 16
SCOTLAND V NORWAY
Tuesday June 23
SCOTLAND V MOROCCO

Colin Hendry

Age	Caps	Value
31	28	£3.5 million

Every team needs an inspirational leader in the World Cup finals, a player that can lead his team into the most famous and prestigious tournament in the world with his head held high.In Colin Hendry Scotland have undeniably one of the most influential players in France.

A true Braveheart, the Blackburn defender goes into the Championships riding high after a successful season in the domestic league. He is a marvellous tackler and can beat any attacker to the ball in the air. He will prove to be one of Scotland's most important players.

SCOTLAND

Andy Goram

Age	Caps	Value
33	54	£2 million

Though his place is under threat from old-timer Jim Leighton, Andy still firmly believes that he has what it takes to be the Scotland number one. What he lacks in mobility he makes up for in his outstanding ability at shot stopping.

Andy has had a phenomenal career. After beginning with spells in England he was recognised by Rangers as one of the top Scottish goalkeepers. He has helped Rangers to numerous championships and Scotland to a World Cup place.

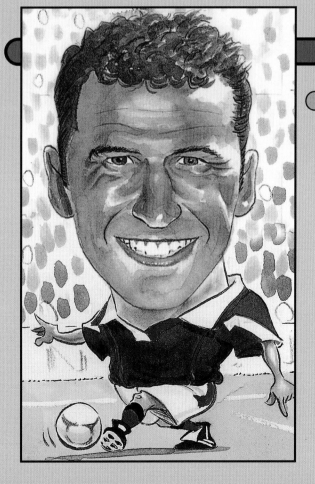

Colin Calderwood

Age	Caps	Value
32	23	£500,000

Colin did not gain international recognition until quite late in his career but has fitted in very well in defence alongside Colin Hendry. He is another who exemplifies the true fighting spirit of the Scottish team with his whole hearted determination and spirit.

The Tottenham defender had an indifferent season leading up to the World Cup but is hoping that, wherever his future lies in the domestic game, he will help Scotland progress in France.

Duncan Ferguson

Age	Caps	Value
26	9	£4.5 million

On his day he is the best in the air in the British game. He causes absolute mayhem when he is in the mood. But 'being in the mood' is big Duncan's major problem.

Although he has not always seen eye-to-eye with Craig Brown and his other managers over the years, there is no doubting his ability. Could prove to be either Scotland's most dangerous weapon or their biggest liability.

Tom Boyd

Age	Caps	Value
31	50	£1 million

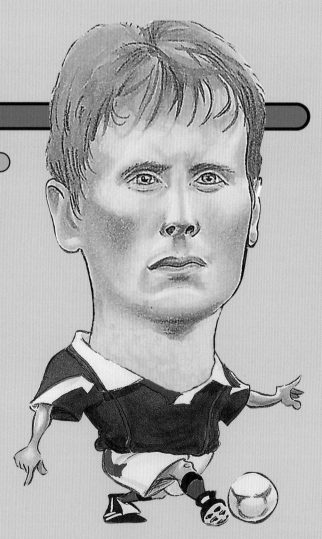

Having passed the 50 cap milestone and previously played in a World Cup, many will look to Boyd to play the role of mentor to the less experienced players in the side.

A left-back who gets forward and defends well there is a question mark over his lack of pace. He scored a rare goal which was vital for qualification and will be hoping for another in France.

Billy Mckinlay

Age	Caps	Value
28	22	£3 million

Billy is another who has prospered since moving to England. He was always thought of as a useful player in his Dundee United days but since arriving at Blackburn he has shown Craig Brown exactly what he is capable of.

A terrier-like midfielder who is always right in the thick of the action, he doesn't venture forward very often but when he does score a goal it is usually spectacular. While his form has improved since moving to Rovers, he seems to have found extra impetus since he changed his hair colour! What next for the fiery Scotsman ?

David Hopkin

Age	Caps	Value
27	4	£4 million

David is a player who has come out of the wilderness and shown everyone around Britain what he can do. When lingering in the Chelsea reserves and during his time at Crystal Palace he did not shine.But George Graham spotted his true determination and skill and bought him for Leeds United in a multi-million-pound deal.

He revealed that he is a quality player not only to the Premiership but to Craig Brown who now sees him as a vital player in Scotland's World Cup campaign. He is quick, has good distribution and packs a powerful shot. If he is in form, Scotland will tick.

Kevin Gallacher

Age	Caps	Value
31	36	£3 million

Kevin has become the regular goalscorer his country has craved. He is quick and deadly in front of goal, attributes that Kevin has had to work at and that have not come as naturally as to many other players.

He has had an outstanding season for Blackburn Rovers scoring over 20 goals. He and the whole of Scotland will be hoping that he can recreate that form for his country.

John Collins

Age	Caps	Value
29	18	£5 million

Undoubtedly Scotland's most talented player. His move from Celtic to French giants Monaco has enhanced his game and added skill, strength and balance to a player of great ability on and off the ball.

Having played in France for two seasons he will feel relaxed in the stadiums that he has graced over the past couple of years. This can only help John and Scotland. If he performs to his potential then Scotland could turn a few heads.

SCOTLAND

Darren Jackson

Age	Caps	Value
31	17	£2 million

After scaring the soccer world with problems with serious injuries, Darren has made a remarkable recovery to full fitness and is fighting for a place in the Scotland first team.

Before his horrific injury he seemed destined to show the Celtic fans that he could play at the highest level and he was riding high in the Scotland first team. Now he is back to square one and it could work in his favour. Having to prove himself to Craig Brown again could add extra effort and extra dimensions to his game.

Gordon Durie

Age	Caps	Value
31	38	£2 million

Another with bagfuls of experience that will be a tremendous bonus to the Scotland squad. Gordon has always been a livewire up front and the years have been kind to him: he has not lost any of his pace or ability.

Gordon never seems to recreate the form which sees him sparkle in the qualifying stages when he gets to the finals. He is determined that this year he can show the world what he can do and not come back disappointed with his own performances.

Profiles of the rest of the squad

Jim Leighton

At 39 Jim will be one of the oldest players going into this World Cup. He is a true Scotsman who on many occasions has saved his team-mates with outstanding performances. He will battle with his good friend Andy Goram for a place in the side.

Christian Dailly

The Derby centre-back is being talked about as a key member of the Scottish defence. Play comes out of the back more smoothly with Christian, who can also play in midfield. Good on the ball, only lack of experience could threaten a first team place.

Matt Elliot

Still to break into the Scotland side, he is a newcomer who is an absolute jewel of a find for Craig Brown. He is now rated as one of the top defenders in Britain; his ability to score and get in great positions could add an extra dimension to the Scottish attack.

Jackie McNamara

Since his move to Celtic Jackie has become a firm favourite with the Scottish fans. He is mobile and has a good footballing mind. What he lacks in height he makes up for in pace.

Craig Burley

Though Craig would feel rather unfortunate to be left out of the Scotland first team regularly he has not played first-team football since his move to Celtic a year ago. He has been in sparkling form for the super hoops and is a midfielder with a real appetite for goals.

Paul Lambert

Along with John Collins, Paul has played abroad for a top European side, Borussia Dortmund, which helps him feel more comfortable on the big occasion. A great player to have in the squad who can play in many positions.

David Weir

David is a talented defender who has broken into the squad but he is not likely to feature in the first team. He travels to France as a squad member and if the Hearts-stopper is called upon, he would do a decent job.

Neil Sullivan

The youngest keeper in the squad and unlikely to play. He has shown in the Premiership that he has a lot of ability; strong in the air and a good shot-stopper.

Scott Gemmill

Once touted as the next best thing since his father, Scott has unfortunately not had a similarly dazzling career . The Forest player is still a talented midfielder who will run all day and has an eye for goal.

Stuart McCall

Stuart is another true fighter who always puts his heart, soul and anything else he can find into the game! He has been a great servant to both club and country over the years and will be a valuable player to have in the camp.

Simon Donnelly

Simon is a young player who could make a name for himself in France. He has shown that he has tremendous skill and pace when playing for Celtic and gives Scotland some much needed youth.

Ally McCoist

One of the great characters of the Scottish game, Ally could well be given his last chance on the international scene. He scored a wonder goal in the European Championships; how he would cherish another in France.

Gary McAllister

Age	Caps	Value
32	56	£2 million

An injury to Gary a third of the way through the 97-98 season saw him lose much match practice and was a major worry for Craig Brown and Scotland. Having probably been the most talented player in the side over the past five years Gary may not have shaken off his injury in time for the World Cup.

Though the emergence of such players as Hopkin, Burley, Collins and Lambert have threatened Gary's place in the side many believe that the Coventry playmaker still has what it takes and can perform at any level.

How they got there

Group 4

Date	Home		Away	Score
01-Jun-96	Sweden	vs	Belarus	5:1
31-Aug-96	Belarus	vs.	Estonia	1:0
31-Aug-96	Austria	vs.	Scotland	0:0
01-Sep-96	Latvia	vs.	Sweden	1:2
05-Oct-96	Estonia	vs.	Belarus	1:0
05-Oct-96	Latvia	vs.	Scotland	0:2
09-Oct-96	Belarus	vs.	Latvia	1:1
09-Oct-96	Sweden	vs	Austria	0:1
09-Nov-96	Austria	vs.	Latvia	2:1
10-Nov-96	Scotland	vs.	Sweden	1:0
11-Feb-97	Estonia	vs	Scotland	0:0
29-Mar-97	Scotland	vs	Estonia	2:0
02-Apr-97	Scotland	vs	Austria	2:0
30-Apr-97	Latvia	vs.	Belarus	2:0
30-Apr-97	Sweden	vs.	Scotland	2:1
30-Apr-97	Austria	vs	Estonia	2:0
18-May-97	Estonia	vs	Latvia	1:3
08-Jun-97	Belarus	vs	Scotland	0:1
08-Jun-97	Latvia	vs	Austria	1:3
08-Jun-97	Estonia	vs	Sweden	2:3
20-Aug-97	Estonia	vs	Austria	0:3
20-Aug-97	Belarus	vs	Sweden	1:2
06-Sep-97	Latvia	vs	Estonia	1:0
06-Sep-97	Austria	vs	Sweden	1:0
07-Sep-97	Scotland	vs	Belarus	4:1
10-Sep-97	Sweden	vs.	Latvia	1:0
10-Sep-97	Belarus	vs	Austria	0:1
11-Oct-97	Scotland	vs	Latvia	2:0
11-Oct-97	Austria	vs	Belarus	4:0
11-Oct-97	Sweden	vs	Estonia	1:0

FINAL STANDINGS

Austria	10	8	1	1	17	4	25
Scotland	10	7	2	1	15	3	23
Sweden	10	7	0	3	16	9	21
Latvia	10	3	1	6	10	14	10
Estonia	10	1	1	8	4	16	4
Belarus	10	1	1	8	5	21	4

World Cup Odds

150/1

BRAZIL

The squad contains many of the players that brought the World Cup back to Brazil 4 years ago. With the additions that have been made they look to be in even better shape.

Mario Zagallo is probably the most experienced manager in the World Cup finals. Having been involved in 4 successful World Cup campaigns, he leads his team into what will almost certainly be his final tournament.

The Brazilians have always been known for their individual talent and in this year's finals they will not be letting anyone down. Players such as Denilson, Djalminha, Romario and Juninho have the quickest feet in the business. Ronaldo is the player on everyone's minds; he has played in three of the toughest leagues and will now face his most difficult task. If he shows the world that he can recreate the form that he has shown for his clubs then there is no doubt he will be touted as the world's greatest player.

No - one matches the Brazilians when it comes to skill and technique, but there is a question mark over their defence and their goalkeeper. In World Cups of old the defence has seemed to go missing at times and in France the present back four doesn't seem to suggest that it will be any different.

They have the players, the ability and the experience but is there the spirit in the camp? This question will be answered come June. They can win the World Cup, but the odds are they will bow out in the final. Not this year !

Group A

Wednesday June 10
BRAZIL V SCOTLAND
Tuesday June 16
BRAZIL V MOROCCO
Tuesday June 23
BRAZIL V NORWAY

Ronaldo

Age	Caps	Value
21	29	£25 million

Undoubtedly the world's most valuable footballer. Ronaldo is the finest player to come from the Brazilian ranks since Pele. He must not let his commercial career interfere with his football, but that is his only worry at present.

His strength, skill and eye for goal are quite frightening - defenders around the world be warned. With the Brazilians being tipped to go all the way again, Ronaldo will spearhead their challenge. This boy's a bit special.

ONE TO WATCH

Romario

Age	Caps	Value
32	51	£5 million

Romario was the star of USA'94 and despite his age he claims he is in the best shape he has ever been in. Many will remember the partnership he struck up with Bebeto 4 years ago, but it will be the Romario-Ronaldo combination that will scare the life out of opposing defenders!

Fast, highly skilled and deadly in front of goal Romario is still one of the world's most exciting players. In recent years he has not always been in the press for the right reasons and will hope that absolutely nothing distracts him from his football in France.

Rivaldo

Age	Caps	Value
26	10	£13 million

Bought as the replacement for Ronaldo at Barcelona, Rivaldo has been more than adequate in his job in filling the world's most outstanding player. It was not until quite recently that he was selected for international duty and will now play a major role in the Brazilian attack.

His deceiving stature enables him to drift past defenders as well as use his impeccable vision to pick out the most stunning passes. He is one of many in the team who can score from free-kicks with ease and will be another player that will terrorise managers when he is seen on the teamsheet.

Mauro Silva

Age	Caps	Value
21	45	£2.5 million

One of the oldest in the squad, Mauro Silva's experience will be vital to the Brazilians, on and off the pitch. Having played in the World Cup success of '94 and being a household name in Spain over the past 4 years, he is widely admired throughout the game.

Strong in the tackle and able to pass the ball with precision and class, he is perfect playing in that role just in front of the defence. Not every Brazilian can be attack minded !

Aldair

Age	Caps	Value
33	54	£2 million

Another who is aiming to make his third World Cup appearance, Aldair is a rock in the centre of the defence. A 'no-nonsense' defender who lets his opposing strikers know he is around with some hefty but fair challenges.

He has found it hard in recent seasons to recreate that same form for Roma that he does for his country. With the Brazilians always being criticised for their defensive frailties Aldair is one of the most important figures in the side.

Juninho

Age	Caps	Value
25	20	£13 million

Though there was a spell when Juninho was not considered for international duty since his move to Spanish giants Athletico Madrid, he has regained his place and is determined to make one of the attacking midfielders roles in the Brazilian starting team his own.

Those who remember him from his Middlesbrough days know he is an extremely talented player. His sudden change of pace and delicious skills leave opponents simply standing. Could prove to be another Brazilian that who will make a name for himself in France.

!!!STOP PRESS!!! Juninho tragically broke his leg and may not be fit for the World Cup finals !!!STOP PRESS!!!

Taffarel

Age	Caps	Value
31	86	£1 million

Though his form for Brazilian giants Athletico Mineiro, has not been consistent, he looks set to play in his third World Cup finals. He has been a marvellous servant to the national team over the years and though he may not always look as though he is fully aware of what is going on, he pulls off some outstanding saves.

This will almost certainly be his last major championships, and he is hoping that he bows out of this World Cup with another winners medal.

THE WORLD'S MOST EXPENSIVE PLAYER

Denilson		
Age	Caps	Value
20	14	£25 million

After the World Cup, Denilson will become the most expensive player in the world when he completes his move to Spanish side Real Betis. An explosive winger who can also play up front, he is another player who will set France on fire.

His performances in Le Tournoi and in the Copa America earned him a first team spot with Mario Zagallo. He has unbelievable ability drifting past players as though they are not there, shooting with immense power and other delightful tricks that are out of this world. Breathtaking!

Cafu

Age	Caps	Value
28	58	£5 million

After years of having to play second fiddle to Jorginho, Cafu has made the right-back spot his own. Once a boyhood prodigy, he has proven right those who tipped him to go all the way. Though he may seem quiet on the pitch he is an outstanding footballer.

He likes to go forward and whips in some tremendous crosses. His speed and agility are two of his main assets, he also shares a great understanding with fellow defender Aldair with whom he has played not only for Brazil but for their club, Roma.

Djalminha

Age	Caps	Value
26	10	£8 million

Another left-sided player who was in the limelight during '97 but has not had quite the same fortune since his move to Spain. He is a midfielder who possesses one of the sweetest left feet in world football, but it really does depend on what sort of mood he is in.

His national team performances coincide with his form for his club, therefore Mario Zagallo hopes Deportivo will be getting the best out of Djalminha by the time the World Cup comes around. If he can keep his temper under control and plays to his highest level he can make a real name for himself in France.

Profiles of the rest of the squad

Carlos Germano

He will go to France, number two to Taffarel, but will almost certainly be handed the number one spot after the World Cup. If called upon, he would hope to regain the form he has been in for club side Vasco de Gama where he has had an outstanding season.

Junior Baiano

Has emerged as one of the favourites to fill one of the roles in the centre of defence. His form for Flamengo has alerted Mario Zagallo and he seems to have curbed his temperament. Another who scorches the net with his shots.

Goncalves

A natural leader on the field, he is one of the few Brazilians not to have played in European football. At 32 he is a latecomer to the national team but will do a job if called upon.

Andre Cruz

The AC Milan centre-back is another candidate to fill the defensive role that is the only worry to Mario Zagallo. He is experienced at international level but has a tendency to let his mind wander at times. Yet another player with a cultured right foot when taking free-kicks.

Ze Roberto

An extremely talented player who can either play in midfield or defence. Playing in Spain he has been noted as a valuable squad player; he is only young and is being groomed to replace Mauro Silva.

Ze Maria

Another youngster who is slowly being given a taste of international football but will not have a first team place in France. He has shown at Parma that he has delightful skills, but he will have to settle for just a place in the squad.

Flavio da Conceicao

He will contest the position of anchor man with Mauro Silva, though will most likely have a place on the bench. He is a destroyer in the midfield who also has accurate distribution and an impressive goalscoring record for club side Deportivo.

Leonardo

Whilst playing in the last World Cup as left-back (infamously being sent off), he goes into France contesting Juninho and Denilson for one of the attacking midfield places. A very intelligent footballer, on and off the ball.

Rai

Though he has captained Brazil on occasions it does not look as though there will be a starting place for him in this year's World Cup. At 32 he still has all the skill and good distribution, but the fitness is going.

Bebeto

Though he partnered Romario 4 years ago, there is now in tough competition for a place in the side. Bebeto has found it hard to settle at a club in the last few seasons, yet he still has what it takes to produce the goods, as shown in his recent performances for the national team.

Roberto Carlos

No doubt Roberto Carlos will be one of the first on Mario Zagallo's team-sheet. In the last 3 years he has shown that he is the best left-back in world football and he will go to his first World Cup with a huge reputation to uphold.

Edmundo

He was top scorer in Brazil the season before last and although his impressive goalscoring record speaks for itself, he is a danger to Mario Zagallo's squad. He was sent off seven times last season and his nickname the 'animal' is quite appropriate. Still a superb striker.

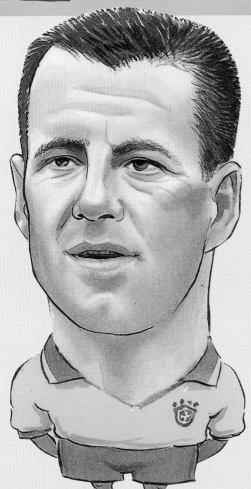

Dunga

Age	Caps	Value
34	56	£1 million

Having captained Brazil to their last World Cup success 4 years ago, he travels with the squad unable to command a place in the side. Even though he may not figure in the starting team he is an absolute must for Brazilian morale. Dunga's inspiration and leadership qualities are envied by many other teams.

Strong in the tackle with delightful little touches he links the pay well and will do a great job if called upon.

How they got there

Qualified as 1994 Champions

World Cup Odds

3/1

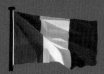
What are their chances ?

France go into the Championships as second favourites, but some unconvincing recent performances has raised questions about the depth of the French squad.

There is no doubt that within the group of players Aime Jacquet has assembled there is some dazzling talent. Zidane, Djorkaeff and Ba are just three players that havethe potential to breach any defence that the French face. The defence and goalkeeper seem sound, and Laurent Blanc will almost certainly inspire much of the young talent around him. Lilian Thuram is another who many strikers will find it difficult to get past. The midfield has a very steady balance with Desailly and Zidane. The problem lies with the attack.

Djorkaeff is undoubtedly France's most consistent striker, though there have been rumblings of discontent concerning his lack of committment in defence, while Djorkaeff and Zidane are too similar to be complimentary. The player who would partner the Inter ace is still a question that many of the French are asking, and even the manager will find it hard to answer. He has a host of strikers whom he can select from: Loko, Dugarry, Guivar'ch, Trezeguet or even the veteran Papin.

Up to the European Championships the French were talked about as having the most settled side in world football. Since then there have been numerous changes and Jacquet has struggled to find a sollution for his attacking problem.

With the home nation expectant the pressure will be felt and the French will find it extremely difficult to deliver. A semi-final place.

ONE TO WATCH

Friday June 12	
FRANCE V SOUTH AFRICA	
Thursday June 18	
FRANCE V SAUDI ARABIA	
Wednesday June 24	
FRANCE V DENMARK	

Zinedine Zidane

Age	Caps	Value
25	28	£10 million

The French public always knew of his genius but it was not until he moved from Bordeaux to Juventus a couple of seasons ago that he showed the rest of the world what he can do. One of the most inventive players on the globe, he is what makes the French team click.

He is quick and mobile. His distribution is close to perfect and his only problem could be that his team-mates rely so much on him for flair and inventiveness that he may disappoint on occasion.

FRANCE

Robert Pires

Age	Caps	Value
24	7	£5 million

The Metz attacking midfielder has made a huge impression on the French coach. He is a silky, skilled player who comes forward to add to the attack and often scores outstanding goals.

There is much interest surrounding Pires and he will be using the World Cup is an opportunity to put himself in the shop window. He has the ability to change a match with a moment of magic and could prove a little gem for the hosts.

Christian Karembeau

Age	Caps	Value
27	29	£5 million

The dreadlocked bombshell is a handful for any opposing defender. Although he is usually called upon for his defensive qualities, when he does come forward his strength seems to enable him to bundle his way through.

After a spell in Italy he now plays his football in Spain, but he has struggled with injury. He will hope to get over any niggles in time for the World Cup, and could play an important role for Aime Jacquet. A powerhouse down the right.

FRANCE

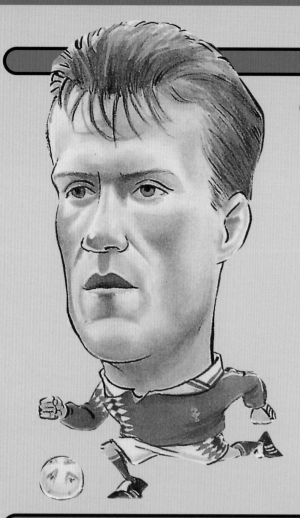

Didier Deschamps

Age	Caps	Value
29	63	£3.5 million

Alongside Zidane and Desailly, Deschamps makes up what is probably the most well-balanced midfield going into the World Cup. Didier is very experienced and will help many of the youngsters in the French squad with their all-round games.

Adored by the French public, Deschamps is one of those players that very rarely have a bad game. Always impressive with his passing, shooting and tackling, he is a complete midfielder.

Youri Djorkaeff

Age	Caps	Value
29	31	£10 million

Youri goes into his first World Cup as the French number one striker. He is a player who has become a household name in France, and now Italy where he has been in tremendous form for Inter Milan over the last few seasons.

With the ball at his feet and speed on his side, there are few defenders who are going to be able to stop the flying Frenchman. A brilliant talent that scores incredible goals and is a threat from in and around the penalty area.

Marcel Desailly

Age	Caps	Value
29	27	£5 million

The 'rock', as he is known in his homeland, will play a major part in the French team if they are to have any success. He has probably been Milan's most consistent player over the past few disastrous seasons.

His nickname reflects his style of play - strong and hard in the tackle. It is not yet known whether he will play in the centre of defence or be used as an anchor man, a role in which he is very effective. Very little gets past the big Frenchman and he is a major asset to the team.

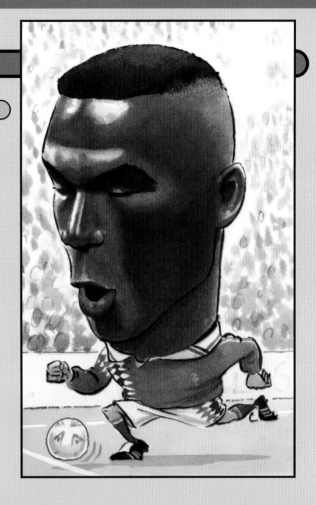

Patrick Vieira

Age	Caps	Value
24	5	£5 million

He may look as though he would be more comfortable on a basketball court, but Patrick's giant stature is well suited to football. He was an unknown when transferred from Milan to Arsenal a few seasons ago, but he is now a full international and is raring to go for the World Cup.

He may not be an automatic choice is still learning but with his astonishing development over the past few years, he will be a very useful squad member.

Frank Leboeuf

Age	Caps	Value
29	11	£4 million

Another who plies his trade in England, Chelsea fans will tell you that he is one of the top defenders in the world, and Aime Jacquet has certainly recognised that he does have plenty of talent.

With good distribution and a tremendous shot he can easily slot into a midfield position, but his height and tackling are his major attributes and make him an all-round defender. Frank may be another who is unsure of a first-team place, but will be determined to make a few appearances.

Lilian Thuram

Age	Caps	Value
25	27	£10 million

There will be much debate over the most promising players coming into this World Cup, but few would dispute the outstanding talent of Lilian Thuram. Having been voted one of the top players in the Italian League, he has to show all of his supporters that he has the ability to perform at the highest level.

Not only can he tackle, pass and position himself to near perfection, he has one of the best temperaments seen in the game for a long time.

Ibrahim Ba

Age	Caps	Value
24	7	£6.5 million

Since his move from Milan he has been somewhat 'on a leash' and he is keen to show what he can do if selected for the French team. He is a scintillating player whose dazzling runs and crosses cause mayhem for opposing defenders.

Although his ability is as good as anyone's going into this World Cup ,Ba needs to be in the mood to be seen at his best. A tendency to change his hair colour sometimes changes his fortunes, so watch out for some outrageous variations come June!

Florian Maurice

Age	Caps	Value
24	4	£8 million

His move to Paris St-Germaine has brought him international recognition, something that many in France have questioned. His time in the capital has seen him score some wonderful goals but also miss some glaring chances.

He is quick and has a real eye for goal but is another player that Aime Jacquet scratches his head about because of his lack of consistency in front of goal. Could prove a hit or a miss.

FRANCE

Bernard Lama

The 34-year-old goalkeeper is in contention for a starting place but lack of match practice makes Aime Jacquet hesitate before naming Lama in his first team. Since a drug-related incident he has not played much first-team football so there remains a question mark over the colourful goalkeeper.

Bixente Lizarazu

Having 30 caps under his belt, he is no stranger to the international scene but is in danger of younger talent filling his role. Still a class act and will probably end up with one of the defensive positions.

Pierre Laigle

The tough-tackling midfielder who can always be called upon to add a bit of bite to the midfield. He has shown that he can play alongside the world's elite with some outstanding performances for Sampdoria.

Bruno N'Gotty

They don't come much stronger than Bruno. The mighty defender has never been a regular for France but is a player who never seems to let his side down. He also packs a powerful shot. Keepers beware.

Emmanuel Petit

Since his move from Monaco to Arsenal he has not seemed to figure in the manager's plans. He is an anchor man who plays either in the centre of defence or midfield. Still a very talented player, though may not figure in Jacquet's first-team plans.

David Trezeguet

The French sensation who has been grabbing all the headlines. At only 20 he seems as though he has pretty much everything a striker needs: pace, strength, awareness and of course an eye for goal. Such precocious talent could be just what France has been lacking in the past 6 months.

Stephane Guivar'ch

Another striker who has had a marvellous season for Auxerre. Having shown what he can do in the domestic league he has yet to prove himself at international level. Another card Jacquet can play.

Patrice Loko

Patrice was one of the most outstanding talents to have come out of the French league, but personal problems have restricted him from really fulfilling his talent in recent years. He is still deadly in front of goal and will be one of, many competing for the striker's role.

Christophe Dugarry

After taking one of the attacking roles for granted it seems Christophe has not been considered as of late. Since his moves from Bordeaux to Milan and then to Barcelona he has not been able to recreate anything like the same form that saw him force his way into the squad three years ago.

Fabien Barthez

He will push Bernard Lama and any other keeper that is considered for the number one shirt. He has had some outstanding performances for both club and country over the past few seasons but there is no assured place for him in the team.

Alain Boghoission

Yet another midfielder who will be on the bench. Alain has never really broken into the first team but there has never been any doubt about his ability. He is one more of the squad who plays away from his home country and many have argued that if he played in France, he would stand a better chance of being selected.

Jean-Pierre Papin

The 33-year-old's international career had looked dead and buried but, with the manager's realisation that he is desperately in need of finding someone to stick the ball in the net, Papin could be Jacquet's man. A legend who may just be given one last chance.

How they got there

Laurent Blanc

Age	Caps	Value
32	63	£1 million

This will most probably see the end of an international career for a hero in the French game. Laurent has been a stalwart over the years for the clubs that he has played for and of course, for his country.

His speed may not be what it used to be but he makes up for his lack of pace with his irrepressible experience. Aime Jacquet is still holding his cards close to his chest over who will be captaining the hosts but Blanc is the favourite, and what a captain marvel he is.

France qualify as hosts

World Cup Odds

13/2

What are their chances ?

Holland have often shown that they are the most technically gifted side in a major tournament but a lack of resilience and strength have always led to their downfall.

Like many managers of Dutch teams of old, Guus Hiddink has his critics, but he showed in the qualifying rounds that he may have added the steel to the side that has been lacking. Hiddink is a quiet character but is very tactically aware and often finds the appropriate formula for each game.

Much of the squad remains the same as it was in the European Championships two years ago and there is a large contingent who played in the USA in the last World Cup. This bodes well, as experience will give the Dutch an advantage over many other sides who go into this World Cup with fairly unproven teams.

A first impression of the squad is that there is a wealth of skill and talent. However, a second glance at these players reveals players who do not always produce the goods on a regular basis. Bergkamp, Overmars, Seedorf and Kluivert are rated as the best in the world on their day but if they do not perform it will be hard to see where the goals are going to come from. Defensively, they are sound and in Van Der Sar they have a strong and dependable goalkeeper. Another to watch out for is Giovanni van Bronckhorst: taking the Dutch league by storm, he will be looking to impress in France.

The Dutch are still lacking the vigour that many of their European counterparts have in their squads and a quarter-final place is as far as they will go.

ONE TO WATCH

Group E

Saturday June 13
HOLLAND V BELGIUM
Saturday June 20
HOLLAND V SOUTH KOREA
Thursday June 25
HOLLAND V MEXICO

Dennis Bergkamp

Age	Caps	Value
28	57	£9 million

Dennis is one of the most gifted players in World Cup this year. He has proved since his move to England that he has what it takes to perform at the highest level.

His form for Holland has not been what he has wanted it to be over the past two years but he is a player who can win matches with a flash of inspiration. Technically wonderful with hints of Cruyff, he is hoping to bring some glory back to the Netherlands.

Arthur Numan

Age	Caps	Value
27	24	£3.5 million

Arthur is now in the prime of his career. There were fears that he would never fulfil the potential but he has shown in recent years that he has got what it takes. He is now seen as a very important player and will prove to be a useful addition to the Dutch squad.

It would seem that his best position is wing-back, playing on either the right or left side. He is strong in the air and on the ground, and poses a problem for opposing defenders and attackers.

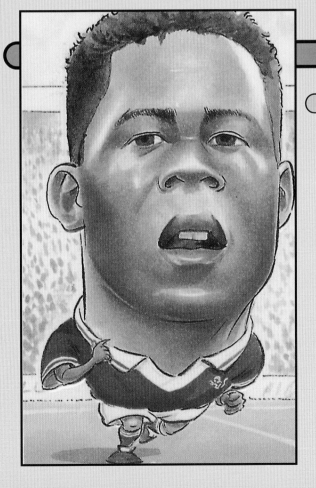

Patrick Kluivert

Age	Caps	Value
21	16	£10 million

Since his move from Ajax to Milan Kluivert has failed to rediscover the form that brought him rave reviews and saw him toted as Holland's new wonder kid. A recent hat-trick has shown doubters that still has the talent to play at the highest level.

He is undeniably a fantastic prospect and could provide the cutting edge that has been missing from the Dutch attack. Not only does he score stunning goals, his strength makes him a formidable all-round attacker.

Clarence Seedorf

Age	Caps	Value
21	26	£8 million

Seedorf is one of the most important players in the Dutch team. Having played in the Dutch, Italian and Spanish league he has the experience of many much older players.

His distribution is perfect and it will be hard to find another player who can pass the ball as naturally. Dreadlocked and dangerous, Clarence could become one of the real stars in France.

Marc Overmars

Age	Caps	Value
25	35	£7.5 million

At 25 years of age Marc seems a veteran at international level. He has proved over the years to be more than a handful for opposing defenders, as many Premiership defences have discovered.

With his strength, speed and crossing ability, he is a perfect winger but also scores goals at both club and international level .

Wim Jonk

Age	Caps	Value
31	39	£2 million

After a glittering career in Italy and Holland, Wim is now almost certain to bow out of the international scene in this World Cup. He is a committed player for both club and country and you can be certain he will put 100% into every game.

His preferred position these days is just in front of the defence. What he lacks in pace he makes up for in great distribution and an ability to score goals from outrageous distances.

Ronald De Boer

Age	Caps	Value
27	36	£4 million

Ronald De Boer is one of the truly outstanding players in the Dutch squad. His versatility and the range of different positions he can play in is extremely valuable. He has always had added recognition for the fact that he and his twin brother, Frank, are currently the most successful brothers in international football.

Ronald is more comfortable in a midfield position and has had another successful season for Ajax.

Edwin van der Sar

Age	Caps	Value
28	21	£3.5 million

Many goalkeepers coming to the World Cup are full of fancy skills and great flamboyancy. Edwin does not usually possess such talents; he is steady and reliable, the two attributes a defence most valued for a defence playing in front of their goalkeeper.

With over 20 caps under his belt, he has the confidence and experience not to falter when the big occasion arises. Many believe that the Dutch have a weak link in the goalkeeper department; Edwin will be hoping to prove them wrong.

Winston Bogarde

Age	Caps	Value
27	10	£5 million

A player who has seen the sights of Europe in the past season, when moved form Ajax to Milan to Barcelona in less than one season!

Playing for such giants of Europe has done his international claims no harm and there is no doubting his defensive ability. He is quick, level-headed and very reliable; an important member of the Dutch team.

Aron Winter

Age	Caps	Value
30	38	£3.5 million

Another who earns his money in Italy where he plays for giants Inter Milan. Aron is often thought of as a veteran at this level, but he plays with such vigour and commitment that one would think he is just starting out.

Whether he plays on the right side of midfield or in the centre, he will apply his skill and determination evenly and consistently. He will probably be used as a squad player where his utility as a link man will prove to be a great asset.

Phillip Cocu

Age	Caps	Value
27	15	£6 million

Phillip is a player who can work magic in the centre of the park. With the news that he is moving to Spain after the World Cup he will hope to prove that he is worth every penny and make a firm stamp on the international scene. Something he failed to do of late.

Whilst playing in Holland he has had a perfect stage to claim a place in the national side, but like many other players in the Dutch midfield he lacks consistency. On his day though, he is a matchwinner.

HOLLAND

Ed De Goey

Since his move to Chelsea he has been unable to reclaim his number one spot but is pressing hard to retain the goalkeeper's jersey. He is an agile and a dominating goalkeeper and could end up playing a part in the Dutch World Cup campaign.

Michael Reiziger

Another Dutchman who did not enjoy Italy too much, but since his move to Spain he has recaptured his form and will go to the World Cup. Probably as a first-team player.

Giovanni Van Bronckhorst

Giovanni is being touted as the new wonder kid of Dutch football. Though he may not feature in the starting eleven, he will give the Dutch team an extra dimension with his flair and skills .

Jaap Stam

A young defender with a bright future in front of him; he has been targeted by many of the top sides in Europe. Extremely mobile and comfortable with both feet, he will be hoping to add a few extra million to his price tag with some decent performances come June.

Jean-Paul Van Gastel

A strong midfielder with plenty of determination and commitment. Jean-Paul will probably not start but has shown in the past few seasons for Feyenoord that he has what it takes to play at the highest level.

Johan De Kock

Veteran Johan has shown in his international career that he can produce his consistently solid club form for the national side. Though he has not always been a regular, he has never let his side down when called upon.

Nordin Wooter

Another to come out of the Ajax youth system, he is hoping to follow in the footsteps of Gullit, Bergkamp and Rijkjaard by making a name for himself in the Dutch team.He has yet to show that he is of true international standard but could be given his chance in France.

Pierre Van Hooijdonk

Pierre will go to France as a player who can give the Dutch team another option, and a dangerous one at that. Not only is he the only traditional target man in the squad, but he is good on the ground and always poses a threat to opposing defences.

Ruud Hesp

Ruud has not been recognised as being of international pedigree until lately, where he has been in sparkling form for Barcelona. He will probably not get a chance but is a very strong and reliable keeper who would do a more than adequate job.

Richard Witschge

Older brother Rob had success in the national team and Richard has now matured enough finally to get his chance. In his early years many believed he was never going to be strong enough but his recent form has proved his doubters wrong and he probably is one of the best all-round midfielders in the Dutch game.

Edgar Davids

An unsuccessful move to Milan saw Edgar lose out in the international team but after some dazzling performances and a new lease of life with Juventus he has a good chance of making an impact in the World Cup. Can be electric!

Frank De Boer

Age	Caps	Value
27	50	£5 million

It is rare that a pair of twins play in a World Cup tournament together. The De Boer twins have had a remarkable career, and Frank just seems to have the edge.

Though they are identical in looks, Frank is more solid and can play in any defensive position. He is also comfortable in the middle of the field. At the age of 27 he is now at the peak of his career and will play an essential part in the Dutch World Cup campaign.

How they got there

Group 7

02-Jun-96	San Marino	vs.	Wales	0:5
31-Aug-96	Wales	vs.	SanMarino	6:0
31-Aug-96	Belgium	vs.	Turkey	2:1
05-Oct-96	Wales	vs.	Holland	1:3
09-Oct-96	San Marino	vs.	Belgium	0:3
09-Nov-96	Holland	vs.	Wales	7:1
10-Nov-96	Turkey	vs.	San Marino	7:0
14-Dec-96	Wales	vs.	Turkey	0:0
14-Dec-96	Belgium	vs.	Holland	0:3
29-Mar-97	Wales	vs.	Belgium	1:2
29-Mar-97	Holland	vs.	San Marino	4:0
02-Apr-97	Turkey	vs.	Holland	1:0
30-Apr-97	Turkey	vs.	Belgium	1:3
30-Apr-97	San Marino	vs.	Holland	0:6
07-Jun-97	Belgium	vs.	San Marino	6:0
20-Aug-97	Turkey	vs.	Wales	6:4
06-Sep-97	Holland	vs.	Belgium	3:1
10-Sep-97	San Marino	vs.	Turkey	0:5
11-Oct-97	Belgium	vs.	Wales	3:2
11-Oct-97	Holland	vs.	Turkey	0:0

FINAL STANDINGS

Holland	8	6	1	1	26	4	19
Belgium	8	6	0	2	20	11	18
Turkey	8	4	2	2	21	9	14
Wales	8	2	1	5	20	21	7
San Marino	8	0	0	8	0	42	0

World Cup Odds

8/1

SPAIN

What are their chances?

When a major tournament comes around such as the World Cup or the European Championships the same old thing is said about the Spanish : that they just cannot perform on the big stage. However, Javier Clemente's team has had an outstanding run of results, only losing two matches in the past four years, and there is much more optimism in the camp this year.

With an abundance of quality in the squad, they possess probably two of the world's most outstanding talents in Raul and De la Pena. Both are able to turn a match in an instant and are widely admired and feared by opposing teams. At the back they are strong with Nadal and Abelardo forming a defensive partnership that is extremely hard to break. Going forward there is an array of talent; the aforementioned Raul with his precocious talent, the hard-working Luis Enrique and Kiko, an underrated forward that will surprise many come June.

It would seem that the Spanish have undoubtedly one of the most imaginative and skilful squads in the World Cup yet there is a question mark over the strength and depth of the team's experience and whether they have the players to come in and take the place of injuries and suspensions. We wait and see.

Though the Spanish are in what some would say is the 'group of death' they have the ability get to the quarter finals and a semi-final place is more than likely, but no more.

Group D

Saturday June 13
SPAIN V NIGERIA

Friday June 19
SPAIN V PARAGUAY

Wednesday June 24
SPAIN V BULGARIA

ONE TO WATCH

Raul

Age	Caps	Value
20	10	£10 million

Raul is being tipped to become one of the stars of France '98. If he can continue the form he has been in for Real Madrid, there is no doubt he will have the whole world raving about him.

One of the most talented players in the game, Javier Clemente has had no qualms about putting him into the full team at such an early point of his career. He has everything - skill, pace, superb distribution and is deadly in front of goal. Infinite amount of potential.

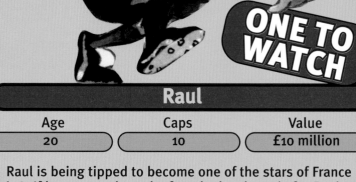

SPAIN

Kiko

Age	Caps	Value
25	18	£6 million

The Spanish have an extremely impressive record going into the World Cup, much of which is down to the form of their new target man. Though Kiko has been in and around the international scene for quite a while, he is now recognised one of the most important players in the side.

A traditional striker who mixes his game with strength and skill. He causes defenders huge problems. Apart from his tremendous power he has extraordinary acceleration.

Juan Caminero

Age	Caps	Value
30	26	£3 million

Juan has played a major part in the Spanish set-up over the past 6 years and it looks as though this World Cup could be his last major championship for his national team.

Whether he plays in his more comfortable attacking role or in a more defensive position, just in front of the back four, he will apply his skill and vision to the team with 100 per cent effort. An inspirational figure for the Spanish team.

Luis Enrique

Age	Caps	Value
27	33	£7 million

One of the most complete midfielders in the game today, Luis is the linchpin in the Spanish side. Everything goes through him, he passes, shoots and tackles with great accuracy: if he is playing well on the day then there is almost a guarantee that the team is going to click.

In Spain he is highly regarded as the key to their success come June. Apart from his awesome presence on the pitch, he is always able to put just that little bit more effort in, though sometimes this can lead him into trouble.

Miguel Angel Nadal

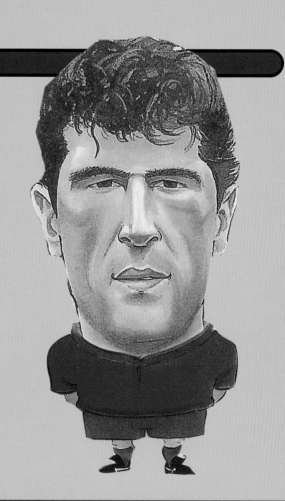

Age	Caps	Value
31	42	£4 million

The 'Beast' as he is more appropriately known in the footballing world was always thought of as Spain's top defender, but in the past year he has not been number one choice at Barcelona and this could see him struggle to hold down a first team place.

Having captained the side and amassed over 40 caps for his country, he is one of the most experienced members of the squad, who will help his team on and off the pitch. A class act, devastatingly strong and very agile.

SPAIN

Ivan De La Pena

Age	Caps	Value
21	3	£8.5 million

Along with Raul, Ivan is Spain's most promising prospect and could make a real name for himself in his first major international Championships. Having broken into the Barcelona first team with such an array of international talent he has learned more than many at his age.

Not only does he win the ball back with such tenacity and commitment, his ability to spot the most ambitious of passes is extraordinary for such a young player. Though he may not be a first team player, he could show the world that Spain has many bright stars ahead.

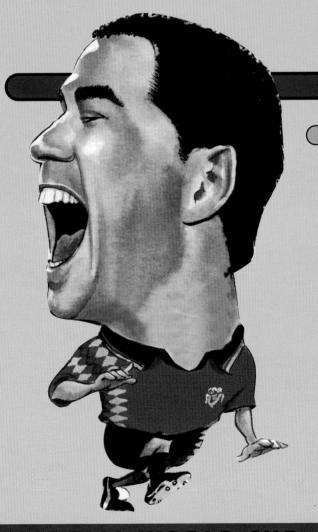

Fernando Hierro

Age	Caps	Value
29	54	£5 million

The driving force in the team, Fernando has proved over the years that at both club and country level he is one of the most complete players in the game. Many believe that much of Real Madrid's success over the past 5 years has come about due to Hierro's form.

With the captain's armband up for grabs, Fernando could well be in line to lead his side into what looks like the hardest group in the World Cup. He will run all day and has a shot that will beat nearly any keeper.

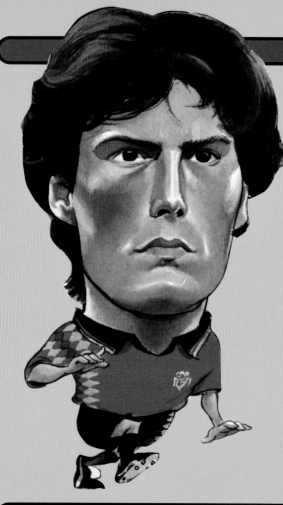

Julen Guerrero

Age	Caps	Value
23	30	£7.5 million

At only 23 Julen is a veteran at international level, but the once touted 'Spanish wonderkid' must now pass his experience of being in the spotlight to colleagues Raul and De la Pena.

His form for his club has not been as outstanding as it was a few seasons ago; which may mean he misses out on a first team place. Whether playing in an attacking midfield position or in a striker's role, he has an abundance of talent and scores spectacular goals.

Santiago Canizares

Age	Caps	Value
28	9	£4 million

Though Andoni Zubizarreta will almost certainly travel with the squad, Canizares looks to start the World Cup in goal for the Spanish. Having had to wait for his chance for many years, he will now try desperately to repeat the marvellous form he has shown for Real Madrid and his country.

He is very agile and often pulls off the most spectacular saves. His consistency could be a problem and the nation of Spain will hold their collective breath to see if he is in the mood to perform on the day.

Barjuan Sergi

Age	Caps	Value
28	30	£6 million

Another squad member who seems to have been on the international scene for a while, Sergi is now in the prime of his career and is hoping that he can recreate the same form he showed throughout Euro'96, where he was undoubtedly one of Spain's best players.

He is comfortable at both left back and left wing-back; he enjoys scurrying forward to tantalise opposing defenders with his small and awkward frame. A certain-starter for the Spanish in their opening matches.

Perez Alfonso

Age	Caps	Value
25	23	£8 million

The rise of Spanish team Betis has had a lot to do with the astonishing performances of their striker Perez Alfonso who has now been able to show that he can produce the goods for his country.

He is very quick and is almost as good with his head as with his feet. He has outstanding ability and uses both feet with devastating consequences for opposing teams. Quite an unknown to many - he will be hoping to change that!

SPAIN

Profiles of the rest of the squad

Andoni Zubizaretta

The veteran goalkeeper will be one of the oldest players going to the World Cup this summer. Still playing in the Spanish Primera, he has maintained his fitness and showed that he is still a class act.

Albert Ferrer

A right-back who has recently been very impressive for the national team. He has great ability on the ball and is hard in the tackle, though he is not attack-minded, he will prove to be a reliable player when called upon.

Roberto Rios

A reasonably new find for the Spanish team, Roberto has come through the ranks and is now looking to play a major part in these Championships. A defensive midfield player with an exquisite touch.

Josep Guardiola

Every season the writers in the Spanish league write off Josep, but he keeps coming back and has been as ever impressive for Barcelona in the past year. He now plays in the role in front of the back four and though may not have the fitness to play a whole game he is more than useful to have in the squad.

Guillermo Amor

Another stalwart in the Spanish team that, on his day, can be a match winner. Whether playing on the wing or through the middle, a pass from Amor can split a defence and win a game.

Emilio Amavisca

Emilio has never been a regular in the Spanish side, but has always impressed whenever called upon. He can use both feet with equal effect and can slot into most attacking positions.

Oli Alvarez

Only in the last season has Oli been recognised as having what it takes to step up to international level. Having formed a deadly partnership with Alfonso for Betis in the last year, he has forced his way into the squad.

Juan Pizzi

Before the European Championships of '96 many billed Pizzi as the star of Spain after finishing as top scorer of the Spanish league... he failed to impress. Since then he has been inconsistent whilst playing for Barcelona but is still a quality striker who can cause many problems for opposing defences.

Jose Molina

The third choice keeper, he will travel in the desperate event of anything happening to Canizares or Zubizaretta. Molina is a solid goalkeeper and his time may come to show what he can do at national level.

Juan Manjarin

Juan is a versatile player who can play in pretty much any position on the park. He is a latecomer to the national side but has put in some gritty performances and could well figure at some stage.

Gonzalez Fran

Fran is another player who has plenty of international pedigree and an abundance of experience at the top level. He may not be able to put in the same sort of effort that he used to, but he is a useful player to have in the squad and would add spirit and morale.

Raphael Alkorta

A strong and stylish defender who likes to bring the ball out of defence. Once thought of as one of the top defenders in the Spanish game, he has not been playing to the best of his capabilities of late and will struggle to get in the side.

Fernandez Abelardo

Age	Caps	Value
27	37	£5 million

A defender who can play in several different positions along the backline. He is very cool headed, he always seems to be in control of the situation. There are times where he seems too casual, but more often that not he comes out on top, even against the best opposition.

He has been a consistent figure in the Spanish squad for many years now and has played in a few major tournaments, so he is an experienced figure for youngsters to look up to.

FINAL STANDINGS

How they got there

Group 6

Date	Home		Away	Score
24-Apr-96	Yugoslavia	vs.	Faroe Islands	3:1
02-Jun-96	Yugoslavia	vs.	Malta	6:0
31-Aug-96	Faroe Islands	vs.	Slovakia	1:2
04-Sep-96	Faroe Islands	vs.	Spain	2:6
18-Sep-96	Czech Republic	vs.	Malta	6:0
22-Sep-96	Slovakia	vs.	Malta	6:0
06-Oct-96	Faroe Islands	vs.	Yugoslavia	1:8
09-Oct-96	Czech Republic	vs.	Spain	0:0
23-Oct-96	Slovakia	vs.	FaroeIslands	3:0
10-Nov-96	Yugoslavia	vs.	Czech Republic	1:0
13-Nov-96	Spain	vs.	Slovakia	4:1
14-Dec-96	Spain	vs.	Yugoslavia	2:0
18-Dec-96	Malta	vs.	Spain	0:3
12-Feb-97	Spain	vs.	Malta	4:0
31-Mar-97	Malta	vs.	Slovakia	0:2
02-Apr-97	Czech Republic	vs.	Yugoslavia	1:2
30-Apr-97	Malta	vs.	Faroe Islands	1:2
30-Apr-97	Yugoslavia	vs.	Spain	1:1
08-Jun-97	Faroe Islands	vs.	Malta	2:1
08-Jun-97	Yugoslavia	vs.	Slovakia	2:0
08-Jun-97	Spain	vs.	Czech Republic	1:0
20-Aug-97	Czech Republic	vs.	Faroe Islands	2:0
24-Aug-97	Slovakia	vs.	Czech Republic	2:1
06-Sep-97	Faroe Islands	vs.	Czech Republic	0:2
10-Sep-97	Slovakia	vs.	Yugoslavia	1:1
24-Sep-97	Malta	vs.	Czech Republic	0:1
24-Sep-97	Slovakia	vs.	Spain	1:2
11-Oct-97	Malta	vs.	Yugoslavia	0:5
11-Oct-97	Spain	vs.	Faroe Islands	3:1
11-Oct-97	Czech Republic	vs.	Slovakia	3:0

Team	P	W	D	L	F	A	Pts
SPAIN	10	8	2	0	26	6	26
Yugoslavia	10	7	2	1	29	7	23
Czech Rep	10	5	1	4	16	6	16
Slovakia	10	5	1	4	18	14	16
Faroe Islands	10	2	0	8	10	31	6
Malta	10	0	0	10	2	37	0

World Cup Odds

14/1

What are their chances ?

Italy have reached the World Cup final 13 times but this year many are doubting Cesare Maldini and his side. After some extremely unconvincing performances, it would seem that the squad is in disarray and lacking morale.

Along with Brazil they have the most talented squad, there is no doubting that, yet there is little camaraderie which is always a vital ingredient to a squad facing a major tournament. Though it may seem from the outside that there is a lack of organisation, Cesare Maldini is a cunning manager and he likes to let his team to the talking.

Many of the players have played together for a while now and there is no new and outstanding prospect that will figure in the first team like many of their rivals have within their ranks. But players such as Del Piero, Inzaghi, Vieiri and Zola would get into any team and are full of talent. Much relies on the midfield that is so constantly scrutinised by the Italian press. Albertini and Di Matteo must prove that they can recreate the same magic for their country.

Though they are criticised they have a superb line-up of players and with a reasonably easy group they will progress. A semi-final place.

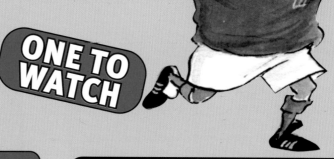

ONE TO WATCH

Group B

Thursday June 11 **ITALY V CHILE**
Wednesday June 17 **ITALY V CAMEROON**
Tuesday June 23 **ITALY V AUSTRIA**

Alessandro Del Piero

Age	Caps	Value
23	16	£20 million

At the prime age of 23 there is still so much more to come from Alessandro Del Piero. Though there have been glimpses of what he is able to do, he has not consistently performed for his national side - many believe this World Cup could be his time to shine.

The Italian press and various lucrative boot deals may seem at times to take Alessandro's mind off the game, but when he is on the ball there are very few players in the world who can match him. The diminutive Del Piero has outstanding ability and is riveting to watch. Could be the star of France'98.

Antonio Benarrivo

Age	Caps	Value
29	23	£3 million

A versatile and solid defender with a lot of experience behind him. He is thought of as one of the most consistent defenders in the Scudetta, having had an illustrious career with Parma.

Cesare Maldini is unsure about his defence and has shown in recent games that there is room for players to come in and prove themselves. Antonio is hoping that he has done enough over his career to gain a place in the starting line-up.

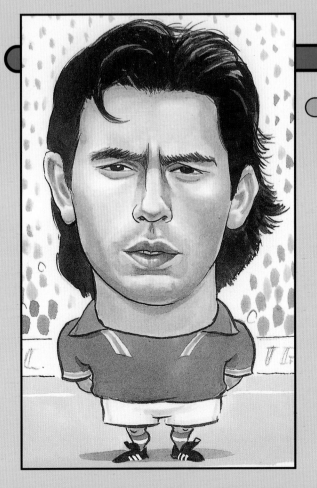

Filippo Inzaghi

Age	Caps	Value
24	3	£10 million

Two seasons ago Filippo made a name for himself scoring freely for Atalanta. Now at Juventus he has taken the leap to one of the biggest clubs in the world in his stride - a quality that all international strikers must show.

With little international experience under his belt he goes into the World Cup purely on his ability. He is highly skilled and has the knack of being in the right place at the right time; another quality of a top striker. It could just be too early for him to show what he can do.

Roberto di Matteo

Age	Caps	Value
27	29	£6 million

It was felt in Italy that when Roberto flew across the Channel to play for Chelsea his international career would be in jeopardy, but after consistently putting in some sparkling performances it has only increased his chances of stabilising his place in the national team.

He is an all-round midfielder: superb distribution, a bite in the tackle and able to score some spectacular goals. He is very important to the team and he just hopes that he can stay free of injury to play a part in what could be a memorable World Cup campaign.

Demetrio Albertini

Age	Caps	Value
26	49	£7 million

Another who plays a vital role in the Italian team, Demetrio has a lot of pressure on his shoulders being the main supplier of goals and also covering back to help an ageing defence.

He is now in the prime of his career and many feel that he could be the most important figure in the Italian side. It is thought that when Albertini is on form the whole team clicks, he and his manager hope that he does not pick up any of the injuries that halted his season last year.

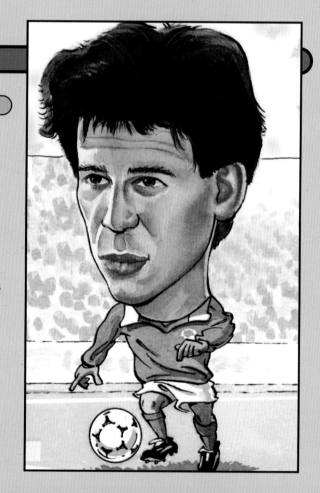

Angelo Peruzzi

Age	Caps	Value
27	20	£4 million

After stealing the number one spot from Gianluca Pagliuca a few seasons ago, he has been irrepressible in goal and looks to stay there for quite a while. In recent years he has been one of the main reasons why Juventus have been so triumphant, though he very rarely gets many of the plaudits.

Some may feel that he flaps at the ball, but he cunningly punches the ball instead of catching it to instantly release an attack, something that many keepers wouldn't dream of doing. Extremely underrated and one of the best number one's in the game today.

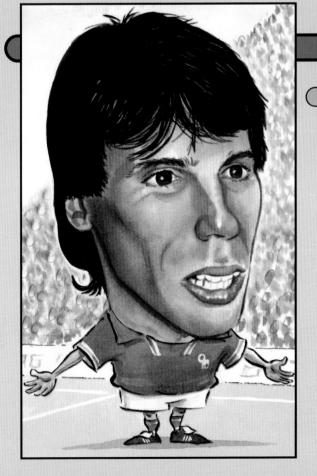

Gianfranco Zola

Age	Caps	Value
31	35	£5 million

A season ago no one would have doubted Gianfranco's place in the team but after a season for Chelsea when he was not in the best of form there could be a question mark over his fitness and his frame of mind.

Undeniably a genius with the ball; his diminutive figure along with a stocky build makes it almost impossible to tackle him. He will hope that come June his form for Chelsea improves and that he can sparkle in what will surely be his final World Cup finals.

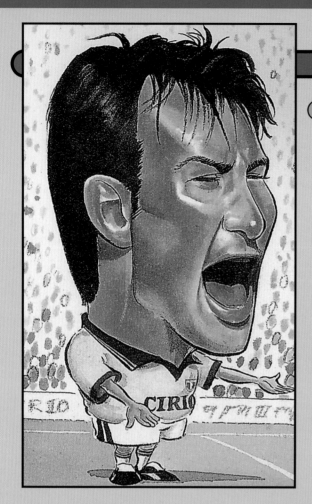

Pierluigi Casiraghi

Age	Caps	Value
28	50	£3.5 million

Now passing the 50 cap mark, Pierluigi is hoping to carry on his impressive international career. Many pundits around the world have always doubted his potential at international level but he has responded with true fighting spirit and a determination to prove them wrong.

He is an awkward player for opposing defenders to play against; tall and robust he causes as many problems in the air as on the ground, for a big man he has a sweet touch.

Dino Baggio

Age	Caps	Value
26	44	£5 million

Dino was probably the most impressive player for the Italian team in the World Cup in America but has failed to build on that in recent years. He has not been able to hold down a first team place yet is not completely disregarded and is thought of as an important member of the squad.

Playing either on the right side or through the middle of the midfield, he is equally able to make an impact with his delightful skill and exquisite passing.

Attilio Lombardo

Age	Caps	Value
31	18	£2 million

The bald eagle made one of the most surprising moves of the season last year when he joined Crystal Palace. Many thought that he was taking a downward step and his international career would be over, but despite having been laid off for a while with injury he has been in quite outstanding form.

Cesare Maldini believes that Attilio has what it takes and that his experience in the English game has only improved his ability. He may not start in the team but will be an extremely valuable player in the squad.

Alessandro Costacurta

Age	Caps	Value
31	51	£2 million

Stylish and composed, he is an example to many youngsters and his defensive qualities are hard to match. His experience in the game is now second to none - having won several trophies with AC Milan and gaining over 50 caps for his country.

Not only is his tackling simply superb but he is also a great organiser and it is always felt that much of the Italian team's simple and competent football comes from the back and especially from Alessandro Costacurta. One of the most important players in the team.

Profiles of the rest of the squad

Gianluca Pagliuca

Once touted as one of the best goalkeepers in the world, he has not recovered from a bad spell of form a few years ago and is now unable to regain his place in the side. Still a very agile keeper who is more than capable.

Ciro Ferrara

Both for Juventus and Italy he has been an absolute rock in the defence and will go down as one of Italy's most reliable players ever. His determination and commitment is hard to match though he does not enjoy the fitness that he used to.

Alessandro Nesta

Alessandro has been tried in the defence recently and has impressed, though it does not look is though he will figure in the starting line-up. A very competent defender who very rarely feels the pressure.

Christian Panucci

One of the rare Italians to make a move to a Spanish club where he has seen success. A terrific little player who, whilst playing at right-back, gets forward and often gets into some great goalscoring positions.

Gianluca Pessotto

A utility man who has recently been brought into the squad after Maldini's observation that there was a lack of bite in the midfield. He is just as comfortable on the left as in the middle.

Antonio Conte

Another of the Juventus contingent in the squad, Antonio is a midfilder who would probably get into most other teams in this World Cup. Although the abundance of talent in midfield will almost certainly deny him a place in the starting line-up, he should figure at some point.
A real terrier.

Angelo di Livio

A player who has shown over the years that he sometimes allows his temperament to get the better of him. Still, he is very effective down the right wing and can also play at full-back.

Enrico Chiesa

His form for Parma has not been as prolific as it was a few seasons ago but he has shown the potential that had so many raving about him a few years ago. He could well be given a chance as Cesare Maldini likes to experiment with his forward line.

Christian Vieri

His move to Athletico Madrid has been reasonably successful, seeing him continue the goalscoring feats he achieved at Juventus. Has not been in favour of late but he is a deadly finisher and an extremely difficult defender to handle.

Gianluigi Buffon

One of the most outstanding prospects, though will probably not be given his chance this summer. He is an outstanding goalkeeper who was playing in the Scudetta at only 18 for Parma. Widely admired around the world.

Fabio Cannavaro

A solid defender with some international experience behind him, yet he will probabaly be used as a squad player. Very mobile and a good man-to-man marker, he will be useful to Maldini if needed.

Luigi Sartor

A very impressive defender who has been in the limelight for Inter Milan this year. Having had such a glittering season on the domestic scene many have tipped him to go on and win a place in the Italian defence, but he may just miss out to more experienced players.

How they got there

Paolo Maldini

Age	Caps	Value
29	85	£7.5 million

Now going into his third World Cup final, he is undoubtedly one of the most accomplished defenders in the world. Once voted the best defender on the globe, recent form has not matched what it was in his mid twenties.

Italian fans will hope that he plays in his more preferred left-back role, as some of his performances at the heart of the defence have not been up to standard. On his day he is unbeatable and difficult to get past, but many wonder that he may just lack some effort due to a certain someone being the manager - his father!

FINAL STANDINGS

Group 2

Date	Home		Away	Score
01-Sep-96	Moldova	vs.	England	0:3
05-Oct-96	Moldova	vs.	Italy	1:3
09-Oct-96	Italy	vs.	Georgia	1:0
09-Oct-96	England	vs.	Poland	2:1
09-Nov-96	Georgia	vs.	England	0:2
10-Nov-96	Poland	vs.	Moldova	2:1
12-Feb-97	England	vs.	Italy	0:1
29-Mar-97	Italy	vs.	Moldova	3:0
02-Apr-97	Poland	vs.	Italy	
30-Apr-97	England	vs.	Georgia	2:0
30-Apr-97	Italy	vs.	Poland	3:0
31-May-97	Poland	vs.	England	0:2
07-Jun-97	Georgia	vs.	Moldova	2:0
14-Jun-97	Poland	vs.	Georgia	4:1
10-Sep-97	England	vs.	Moldova	4:0
10-Sep-97	Georgia	vs.	Italy	0:0
24-Sep-97	Moldova	vs.	Georgia	0:1
07-Oct-97	Moldova	vs.	Poland	0:3
11-Oct-97	Georgia	vs.	Poland	3:0
11-Oct-97	Italy	vs.	England	0:0

PLAY OFFS

Date	Home		Away	Score
29-Oct-97	Russia	vs.	Italy	1:1
15-Nov-97	Italy	vs.	Russia	1:0

England	8	6	1	1	15	2	19
Italy	8	5	3	0	11	1	18
Poland	8	3	1	4	10	12	10
Georgia	8	3	1	4	7	9	10
Moldova	8	0	0	8	2	21	0

World Cup Odds

8/1

GERMANY

What are their chances?

Germany still have the same nucleus of the side that went to the World Cup 4 years ago and won the European Championships in 96 - will this work in their favour or does it mean that much of their squad is going stale?

Berti Vogts is a manager who never seems to be ruffled by pressure and firmly believes that he has the strongest squad of players going into France. He sets firm discipline and it is thought that he has the full respect of all his players, which is of vital importance to a squad which has its sights set on taking the World Cup home with them.

The first team does not seem as strong as some of the others, but Vogts is firm in his belief that he has the deepest and most experienced squad. He would not be wrong in thinking he has the squad who are adept at international football. Sammer, Klinsmann, Hassler, Moller and Helmer are names of a few that are recognised football giants. Many managers can only dream of having such players at their disposal.

Though there is talent in more youthful players such as Dieter Hamann and Lars Ricken these might just not be enough to bring another World Cup back to Germany. By the later rounds some of the legs of the older players may go. A semi-final place.

ONE TO WATCH

Group F

| Monday June 15 |
| GERMANY V USA |

| Sunday June 21 |
| GERMANY V YUGOSLAVIA |

| Thursday June 25 |
| GERMANY V IRAN |

Matthias Sammer

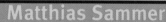

Age	Caps	Value
30	51	£5 million

Matthias is probably the best in the world at what he does on the football pitch. He has one of the coolest heads in the game and he never seems to be under pressure. He arrives in France determined to help the Germans to get their hands on another World Cup.

Managers around the world envy Berti Vogts having such a unique player in his backline. Not only does Matthias have pin-point tackling and perfect positioning, he has the amazing ability to bring the ball out of the defence and turn difficult situations into attacking moves.

Thomas Helmer

Age	Caps	Value
32	63	£2 million

With Sammer, Thomas has built probably the most reliable defensive partnership going into the World Cup. Thomas's reputation precedes him and having played for the two top clubs in German football, he has all the experience a top defender can need.

Even though he is not as young as many of the defenders going into this World Cup, he is still just as fit as he was 4 years ago - and is just as reliable. Devastatingly tough in the tackle, better beware opposing strikers !

Stefan Kuntz

Age	Caps	Value
34	25	£1 million

Though he has never really been able to force his way into a regular first team spot, he has been a great servant to the national team and will go to France in the hope that he can bow out on his international career in style.

Stefan is a versatile player who is able to lay in various positions in the attacking role. He has great body strength and what he lacks in pace he makes up in power and prowess.

Andreas Moller

Age	Caps	Value
30	73	£4.5 million

Andreas is another of the German squad who is very experienced and will not feel the pressure of the big competition as much as many others will. Having played in Italy as well as the top level of the German game with Borrussia Dortmund, he is more than well equipped to take on any team.

He has shown in recent years that he has not lost any of his talent and is still one of the most complete midfielders in the European game. 'Andy' will run all day, his passing, tackling and shooting are all of the highest standard.

Thomas Hassler

Age	Caps	Value
31	88	£2 million

Though it could well be Thomas's last international tournament, there is no doubt that he can look back at a glittering international career. He really stamped his mark on the world scene 8 years ago in the Italian World Cup and has become a firm favourite with the German fans.

He is another in the squad who has played in Italy, which has helped him with his all-round game. He may not be guaranteed of a first team place, but will definitely play a part. He has dazzling skills and his work-rate is first class.

Andreas Kopke

Age	Caps	Value
35	48	£1 million

A very agile and athletic goalkeeper who is of great importance to the German squad both on and off the pitch. He has shown over the years that his inspiration and influence on the side really can change matches.

Andreas did not come into international recognition until quite late in his football career, but even though he will almost certainly be the oldest in the squad he lacks nothing in match fitness and, more importantly, ability.

Stefan Reuter

Age	Caps	Value
31	64	£2 million

Over the past seven years there are very few who have been as consistent in their particular position as Stefan Reuter. Stefan has never let his side down, whether playing for club or country, he always puts in 110% effort.

At the age of 31, he is yet another member of the German squad who will be looking to put that extra bit of effort in as it could well be his last World Cup. Comfortable at either right back or on the left, he is strong in the tackle and his exploits further up the pitch usually result in danger for the opposing team.

Mario Basler

Age	Caps	Value
28	26	£4 million

With many of the German squad selected for their strength and ability , Mario adds some flair and delightful skill. After taking a while to get used to international football, Mario is now more than comfortable playing on the biggest stage in the world.

Not only does he add a certain eloquence to the team, he is also versatile; whether playing on either wing, or through the middle - or even up as a striker - he always seems to perform.

Mehmet Scholl

Age	Caps	Value
27	15	£5 million

Mehmet is one of the most naturally gifted players in the German squad and he is just starting to reach his peak showing great form for both his club and country.

Another player who was recognised late for the national side, rave reviews and outstanding performances for Bayern Munich gave Berti Vogts no choice but to pick this talented midfielder. His deceiving stature helps him drift past players and he also sees passes that many others would not even think about.

Oliver Bierhoff

Age	Caps	Value
29	9	£8 million

Since his remarkable entry into the European Championships final where he scored the winning goal, Oliver has produced outstanding performances both for club and country.

Those who doubted his potential are now silent whilst Oliver is showing the rest of the world how to stick the ball in the back of the net. A strong and powerful front man who not only holds the ball up with such strength, he is quite emphatic in front of goal.

Christian Ziege

Age	Caps	Value
25	24	£7.5 million

At under-21 level Christian was being tipped to become one of Germany's most exciting players and he is certainly living up to that potential.

The 'Z' man now earns his living playing for giants AC Milan, and the Italians only wish he could play for their national team! Whether playing in his more preferred left wing-back position or through the middle, he has pin-point distribution and a very good goalscoring record. A real danger and a player to watch out for.

GERMANY

Profiles of the rest of the squad

Oliver Kahn

Although Oliver may not get the nod over Andreas Kopke there is no doubt about his ability. He could well figure in the World Cup Championships as Berti Vogts had shown before that he is more than willing to give him a chance.

Jurgen Kohler

Veteran defender Jurgen travels to France unsure about his place in the side after some unsteady performances for both club and country. He has all the experience that is needed and will do a job if called upon.

Markus Babbel

Markus could well figure in the first team, but he is another who has not been in the best of form over the past season. He is quick and strong in the air and on the ground.

Christian Worns

A player who has recently been called up to the squad and has a good chance of playing. A traditional centre-back; firm, tall and strong in the air - he does not like to lose the ball.

Dieter Hamann

The wonderkid of German football at present, Dieter cannot seem to put a foot wrong. A lively player with a sweet left foot, many believe that he could make a name for himself in France, but it could just be too early.

Lars Ricken

Quick, determined and inconsistent are three words to describe this Dortmund striker. Undeniably he has what it takes for playing at the top level for both club and country, but his inability to perform consistently has not led him to a first team place. Could be a potential matchwinner.

Thomas Strunz

Thomas epitomises much of what German football is about. Though not the most skilful of players, his manager can always depend on him and he is perfect for the role of playing in front of the back four.

Fredi Bobic

Another who will be ready to hop off the substitutes bench if called upon. The Stuttgart striker is very highly rated in the German domestic league but has never been able to recreate the same form for his country.

Ulf Kirsten

With the rise and rise of Bayern Leverkusen over the past few seasons, the form of Ulf Kirsten has been of great benefit to both club and country. He has been behind Andreas Moller in the pecking order, yet with Moller not getting any younger Ulf could well be given his chance.

Stefan Freund

Hard in the tackle and with an eye for a decisive pass, Stefan is a player that could well come in useful for the German side. The Dortmund midfielder is equally effective on the right or through the centre of the midfield.

Dieter Eilts

After an illustrious international career, Dieter could find himself left out in the cold this summer. He has been magnificent for Germany over the years, especially throughout Euro'96, but Berti Vogts may not be able to find a place for him in his team.

Lothar Mattheus

One of the most talented footballers of the 90s, Lothar could play a part in the German side of 98 at the age of 37. Though his pace and fitness are not what they used to be, he still has all the vision and style that he always had.

Jurgen Klinsmann

Age	Caps	Value
33	100	£2 million

The irrepressible Jurgen Klinsmann leads his country into his final international tournament, opposing teams beware.

Having had one of the most successful careers in World football in recent years, Jurgen will be looking to bow out of the national team with a bang!

The last season did not prove to be as successful as he would have hoped. After an unsuccessful spell in Italy and a less than fruitful return to Tottenham, he will be even more fired up to show the rest of the world that he is still one of the best. Still deadly and of tremendous ability.

FINAL STANDINGS

How they got there

Group 9

31-Aug-96	Northern Ireland	vs.	Ukraine	0:1
31-Aug-96	Armenia	vs.	Portugal	0:0
05-Oct-96	Northern Ireland	vs.	Armenia	1:1
05-Oct-96	Ukraine	vs.	Portugal	2:1
09-Oct-96	Albania	vs.	Portugal	0:3
09-Oct-96	Armenia	vs.	Germany	1:5
09-Nov-96	Albania	vs.	Armenia	1:1
09-Nov-96	Germany	vs.	Northern Ireland	1:1
09-Nov-96	Portugal	vs.	Ukraine	1:0
14-Dec-96	Northern Ireland	vs.	Albania	2:0
14-Dec-96	Portugal	vs.	Germany	0:0
29-Mar-97	Northern Ireland	vs.	Portugal	0:0
29-Mar-97	Albania	vs.	Ukraine	0:1
02-Apr-97	Ukraine	vs.	Northern Ireland	2:1
02-Apr-97	Albania	vs.	Germany	2:3
30-Apr-97	Armenia	vs.	Northern Ireland	0:0
30-Apr-97	Germany	vs.	Ukraine	2:0
07-May-97	Ukraine	vs.	Armenia	1:1
07-Jun-97	Ukraine	vs.	Germany	0:0
07-Jun-97	Portugal	vs.	Albania	2:0
20-Aug-97	Ukraine	vs.	Albania	1:0
20-Aug-97	Northern Ireland	vs.	Germany	1:3
20-Aug-97	Portugal	vs.	Armenia	3:1
06-Sep-97	Armenia	vs.	Albania	3:0
06-Sep-97	Germany	vs.	Portugal	1:1
10-Sep-97	Albania	vs.	Northern Ireland	1:0
10-Sep-97	Germany	vs.	Armenia	4:0
11-Oct-97	Portugal	vs.	Northern Ireland	1:0
11-Oct-97	Germany	vs.	Albania	4:3
11-Oct-97	Armenia	vs.	Ukraine	0:2

Germany	10	6	4	0	23	9	22
Ukraine	10	6	2	2	10	6	20
Portugal	10	5	4	1	12	4	19
Armenia	10	1	5	4	8	17	8
N Ireland	10	1	4	5	6	10	7
Albania	10	1	1	8	7	20	4

World Cup Odds

7/1

What are their chances ?

Under-fire manager Daniel Passarella eventually came through the qualifying rounds after an early scare. The dispute with top player Gabriel Batistuta seems to have been resolved and it looks as though he will be leading the attack.

Gabriel is crucially important: not only is he one of the top goalscorers in Italy for his club but he has a marvellous record for his country. When he performs it seems as though the team takes confidence from him. Alongside him could be the new find, Hernan Crespo; this strike force is Passarella's best hope for success.

Throughout the team there are many fine players who have experience at international level which is always a bonus. Yet many question the spirit in the squad and there is a lingering cloud over the team that once boasted Diego Maradona.

Argentina need a face-lift and after the World Cup a change of manager is on the cards, but a quarter-final place is within reach, though the Argentinian tendency to slip up against some of the lesser teams could see some interesting matches.

Group H

Sunday June 14
ARGENTINA V JAPAN

Sunday June 21
ARGENTINA V JAMAICA

Friday June 26
ARGENTINA V CROATIA

ONE TO WATCH

Gabriel Batistuta

Age	Caps	Value
28	54	£10 million

Gabriel has been the outstanding Argentinian player over the last four or five years. He has shown that he can recreate the same form internationally that has seen him become one of the prolific goalscorers in the Italian Scudetta.

After another superb season for Fiorentina his confidence is riding high and he is hoping that he can continue his rich vein of form. He is strong and powerful in and around the area; he scores both spectacularly and regularly and is one of the most feared strikers in the world.

Javier Zanetti

Age	Caps	Value
24	29	£5 million

Though he has suffered from injury in the past few seasons, there is still no doubting his ability. He is a player who seems to have the legs to run all day, storming up the right wing, delivering crosses and covering back.

Although he is used at a right wing-back position at club level he is preferred at right midfield for his country where he is allowed to go forward more. Extremely quick, he just hopes that he can recover from injury in time to perform in the World Cup.

Jose Chamot

Age	Caps	Value
28	32	£3 million

A hard man in the centre of the defence, Jose will be vital to Argentina if they are to succeed in the World Cup. In recent years the team has lacked balance at the back and Jose has not always been consistent in his performances, yet when he is on form it does seem that he spreads confidence throughout the team.

He is a versatile player who has plenty of experience from playing in the Italian Serie A over the past few seasons. Whether playing on the right, left or in the centre of defence, fans are guaranteed 100 per cent effort.

Profiles of the rest of the squad

Hernan Crespo

Hernan is now one of the most feared strikers in Italy and has shown in the past year that he has what it takes for the international game. He has matured incredibly in the past few seasons and many are touting him to form one of the most deadly partnerships in France with Batistuta. He is quick, strong and can use both feet with equal effect. His power in the box creates havoc for defenders and there is little way to contain him when Hernan is on form.

Claudio Caniggia

Over the past few seasons Argentina may well have been the bad-boys of football. Ressurected Claudio was one of the chief offenders but has now resumed what looked like a diminishing career and is trying to make amends for some of his antics in the past. Unquestionably an extremely talented footballer who has turned in some of his greatest performances in previous World Cup tournaments. His trademark headband and boyish good-looks will still be on show, along with some flamboyant South American skill.

Carlos Roa

With the goalkeeper's jersey up for grabs Carlos could have done enough to show that he is worthy. Strong and agile, a very competent goalkeeper.

Ignacio Gonzalez

Striving to fulfil his dream, the boyish Ignacio is hoping that he gets a chance come June and will be more than happy with a World Cup cap.

Roberto Ayala

A defender whose all-round game is as good as anyone's, except that he lacks pace. He is nevertheless an important member of the team.

Fernando Caceres

Fernando typifies the South American defender, he is mean and lets very little past him, he must watch his temper.

Hernan Diaz

Central defender who is well respected in the Argentinian game, he is a valuable member of the squad who will make good use of considerable experience.

Nestor Sensini

One of those who appeared in USA '94, his versatility and knowledge of the game is vital to the squad. Strong and delightfully skilful.

Leonardo Astrada

Leonardo has flourished over the past few years and is hoping to continue his fantastic form in the World Cup. Forward-running player who will turn a few heads this summer.

Christian Bassedas

A left-sided player who can play either in defence or in the midfield. Another who plays in his native country but could move after the World Cup.

Marcelo Gallardo

One of the outstanding prospects for Argentina, he is a gifted player who has a good footballing brain and combines strength with skill.

Ariel Ortega

Having had another impressive season in Spain and doing well for Argentina in the qualifying rounds, he could well make the starting line-up.

Juan Veron

The Sampdoria midfielder is another naturally talented player whose skills should delight the crowds. Could be his turn to shine.

How they got there

Diego Simeone

Age	Caps	Value
27	63	£5 million

Unquestionably one of the most talented midfielders in the world, Diego now seems to have added consistency to his list of attributes. In the last two years he has shown that he can play at the highest level while at Athletico Madrid and then Inter Milan.

His ability to play the most audacious passes often pays off, and his vision is superb. He also gets forward to score goals and has a sweet right foot at free-kicks.

South American

24-Apr-96	Argentina	vs.	Bolivia	3-1
24-Apr-96	Columbia	vs.	Paraguay	3-1
24-Apr-96	Peru	vs.	Colombia	1-1
02-Jun-96	Equador	vs.	Argentina	2-0
07-Jul-96	Colombia	vs.	Bolivia	3-1
07-Jul-96	Argentina	vs.	Bolivia	3-1
01-Sep-96	Argentina	vs.	Bolivia	3-1
01-Sep-96	Argentina	vs.	Bolivia	3-1
09-Oct-96	Ecuador	vs.	Colombia	0-1
09-Oct-96	Venezuela	vs.	Argentina	2-5
10-Nov-96	Bolivia	vs.	Colombia	2-2
15-Dec-96	Argentina	vs.	Chile	1-1
15-Dec-96	Venezeula	vs.	Colombia	0-2
12-Jan-97	Uruguay	vs.	Argentina	0-0
12-Feb-97	Colombia	vs.	Argentina	0-1
02-Apr-97	Bolivia	vs.	Argentina	0-1
02-Apr-97	Paraguay	vs.	Colombia	2-1
30-Apr-97	Argentina	vs.	Ecuador	2-1
30-Apr-97	Colombia	vs .	Peru	0-1
08-Jun-97	Argentina	vs.	Peru	2-0
08-Jun-97	Uruguay	vs.	Colombia	1-1
06-Jul-97	Chile	vs.	Colombia	4-1
20-Jul-97	Argentina	vs.	Venezuela	2-0
20-Jul-97	Colombia	vs.	Ecuador	1-0
20-Aug-97	Colombia	vs.	Bolivia	3-0
10-Sep-97	Chile	vs.	Argentina	1-2
10-Sep-97	Colombia	vs.	Venezuela	1-0
12-Oct-97	Argentina	vs.	Uruguay	0-0
14-Nov-97	Argentina	vs.	Colombia	1-1

FINAL STANDINGS

SOUTH AMERICA - ROUND ROBIN QUALIFIERS

Argentina	16	8	6	2	23	13	30
Paraguay	16	9	2	5	21	14	29
Colombia	16	8	4	4	23	15	28
Chile	16	7	4	5	32	18	25

Top 4 teams qualified

World Cup Odds

11/1

BULGARIA

What are their chances ?

After exceeding expectations four years ago and reaching the highest point in Bulgarian football by beating Germany in the quarter-finals many believed that Bulgaria would create one of the most fearsome forces in world football. Unfortunately there has been a steady decline in Bulgarian football in the past few years and it will be a surprise if they are successful in the World Cup.

The quality still remains, but that is half the problem. The players are pretty much the same ones who did so well in America and they are simply too old to have any impact in such a demanding tournament as the World Cup. Stoichkov is still a wonderful player and there is resilience with players such as Ivanov, Yankov, Borimirov and Kishishev. But the lack of players with natural footballing ability will see Bulgaria struggle.

Although there are players of the highest calibre in the starting line-up, almost all of them are coming towards the ends of their careers. They go to France on a high after qualifying from a tough group but are not expecting too much. Looking at the teams in their group they are advised not to expect a lot this year!

ONE TO WATCH

Group D

Friday June 12
BULGARIA V PARAGUAY

Friday June 19
BULGARIA V NIGERIA

Wednesday June 24
BULGARIA V SPAIN

Hristo Stoichkov

Age	Caps	Value
32	68	£2 million

Undeniably the greatest player that Bulgaria has ever had, he is the most important player in the side. His inspiration and wealth of international experience are what the Bulgarian team have thrived on throughout the nineties.

Once thought of as one of the best strikers in European football, Hristo still has the magic to turn a game. However, he has been out of the Barcelona side and has not had too much match practice.

Trifon Ivanov

Age	Caps	Value
32	71	£1 million

At 32 many defenders would feel that they would not be able to cope with the pressure of a World Cup. Trifon Ivanov, though, has kept himself in tremendous shape and is of great importance to the Bulgarian side.

Though on first glance he may look ragged and messy, he is a very competent defender who is full of determination and spirit. At centre-half, Bulgaria posses one of the most experienced defenders going to France.

Yordan Lechkov

Age	Caps	Value
30	44	£3 million

Every World Cup has them; the unknown players who show they are something special in front of the whole world. Yordan was one of those players four years ago.

Since then he has been wanted by many of the top clubs around Europe. He is tremendous on the ball when playing in a role just behind the strikers, is difficult to pick up and a real handful for defenders. Fitness could be a problem.

BULGARIA

Profiles of the rest of the squad

Luboslav Penev

Though his uncle is no longer the coach of the national side 'Lubo's' place seems reasonably assured. His domestic form has dropped dramatically but he is still effective and the Bulgarian side rely on him to cause problems for opposing defences. With over 50 caps under his belt and a wealth of experience in playing in the Spanish Primera, he could have an edge when Bulgaria play against Spain.

Zlatko Yankov

Over the past few years Bulgaria have relied on the defensive partnership of Yankov and Ivanov. Come June, the veteran defenders will again be asked to tackle some of the greatest strikers in the world. Zlatko seems to have improved with age. Though many footballers come into their prime around the age of 27, at 31 he is at the peak of his career. Another player who is vital to the team.

Borislav Mikhailov

Though ridiculed throughout the last World Cup he is a very a competent goalkeeper who is dominating in the area.

Radostin Kishishev

Strong defender who has a wealth of international experience; very reliable and has shown that he is more than capable at the highest level.

Ivailo Yordanov

He can play in various positions throughout the team and gives the side different options. Good on the ball and an accurate passer.

Daniel Borimirov

A highly charged midfield player, Daniel always puts in 100 per cent effort. Tenacious in the tackle and very committed his temper sometimes gets the better of him.

Emil Kostadinov

Emil is a tricky player who has now shown that he can perform in some of the best leagues in Europe. He will be facing tough competition for a starting place.

Ilian Iliev

Central midfielder who will wait in the wings for his chance. A skilful player, though lacks strength and will almost certainly be used as a substitute.

Milen Petkov

Impressive midfield player who is progressing in the game. It could well be his last chance to show top European clubs what they are missing.

Ivailo Petkov

Solid and reliable, he typifies a Bulgarian footballer. He may not be the most highly skilled player but he is extremely hard-working.

Anatoli Nankov

Reserve striker who has little international experience. He has shown in the domestic league that he can score some spectacular goals.

Marian Hristov

Versatile midfielder who is comfortable on either right or left midfield. Has been in impressive form of late and will be looking to make the starting line-up.

Georgi Donkov

Increasingly impressive striker who likes to drop back and play off the striker. One to watch.

Krasimir Balakov

Age	Caps	Value
31	63	£2.5 million

Along with Stoichkov, Krasimir Balakov is one of the few 'flair' players in the Bulgarian side. Though he is no longer a spring chicken, he still possesses the sweet left foot that had so many people raving about him four years ago.

He may lack pace but he makes up for it in the way he reads the game. He gives the Bulgarian side a touch of class, and with several of his team-mates representatives of the principles of gritty and tenacious football, he gives the team much needed flair.

FINAL STANDINGS

Bulgaria	8	6	0	2	18	9	18
Russia	8	5	2	1	9	5	17
Israel	8	4	1	3	9	7	13
Cyprus	8	3	1	4	10	15	10
Luxembourg	8	0	0	8	2	22	0

How they got there

Group 9

Date	Home		Away	Score
01-Sep-96	Israel	vs.	Bulgaria	2:1
01-Sep-96	Russia	vs.	Cyprus	4:0
08-Oct-96	Luxembourg	vs.	Bulgaria	1:2
09-Oct-96	Israel	vs.	Russia	1:1
10-Nov-96	Luxembourg	vs.	Russia	0:4
10-Nov-96	Cyprus	vs.	Israel	2:0
14-Dec-96	Cyprus	vs.	Bulgaria	1:3
15-Dec-96	Israel	vs.	Luxembourg	1:0
29-Mar-97	Cyprus	vs.	Russia	1:1
31-Mar-97	Luxembourg	vs.	Israel	0:3
02-Apr-97	Bulgaria	vs.	Cyprus	4:1
30-Apr-97	Israel	vs.	Cyprus	2:0
30-Apr-97	Russia	vs.	Luxembourg	3:0
08-Jun-97	Bulgaria	vs.	Luxembourg	4:0
08-Jun-97	Russia	vs.	Israel	2:0
20-Aug-97	Bulgaria	vs.	Israel	1:0
07-Sep-97	Luxembourg	vs.	Cyprus	1:3
10-Sep-97	Bulgaria	vs.	Russia	1:0
11-Oct-97	Cyprus	vs.	Luxembourg	2:0
11-Oct-97	Russia	vs.	Bulgaria	4:2

World Cup Odds

50/1

CROATIA

What are their chances ?

A tricky tie against the Ukraine in the qualifying play-off saw the Croatians coolly ease their way into the World Cup finals. Before the European Championships Croatia were thought of as one of the most promising forces in world football; though they have continued to impress, there are question marks about certain areas.

Miroslav Blazevic, a self-confessed chain smoker, does have a squad with a high spirit. The emergence of the Croatian team several years ago saw a side that took extra pride in representing its country.

The squad comprises of some of the most talented footballers in the world: Suker, Prosinecki, Boban and Boksic would walk into any team. In Davor Suker they have an incredible talent who is extremely hard to contain, whether playing as a central striker or dropping off the forward line.

Looking at their group, they should go through to the second phase and, if their players perform to their potential, they could go on from there.

Group H

Sunday June 14
CROATIA V JAMAICA
Saturday June 20
CROATIA V JAPAN
Friday June 26
CROATIA V ARGENTINA

Slaven Bilic

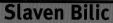

Age	Caps	Value
29	34	£5 million

Very little was known about Slaven when he was brought into the English game by West Ham, but after some very impressive seasons in east London he has had less good fortune since his multi-million-pound move to Everton. Even though last season did not go to plan, he remains vital to the Croatian team. Solid as a rock in the heart of the defence, he could follow many of his national team-mates and move abroad after the World Cup.

Goran Vlaovic

Age	Caps	Value
26	24	£3 million

He will be vying for the striker's role alongside Davor Suker and on current form he could well be in the starting line-up. His form in Spain has been good over the past two years, in fact, much better than was expected.

A nippy forward who likes to take on defenders, his speed is his major asset and allows him to get past the opposition with little difficulty.

Alen Boksic

Age	Caps	Value
27	23	£5 million

Alen has been a prolific goalscorer in Serie A for both Lazio and Juventus but has never been able to reproduce the same form for his country. It has been a problem that makes coach Miroslav Blazevic rack his brains.

Boksic is extremely powerful in and around the box and, on his day, is one of the most difficult players to defend against. Can he finally reproduce his club form on the international stage?

Profiles of the rest of the squad

Davor Suker

Davor, now reaching 30, is still rated as one of the top strikers in European football. The Croatians have become a force to be reckoned with in European football; and much thanks must go to Suker who has been consistently outstanding. For Real Madrid he has shown that he can produce some of the most delightful skills on a football pitch. In Euro '96 he displayed pure magic and showed that the big stage doesn't frighten him. A wonderful player.

Robert Prosinecki

Pivotal player in the Croatian midfield who is so influential on the whole team's performance. He has not been happy in recent years for whichever club he has been at, but his form for his country has remained consistent. Superb playmaker who is always getting involved right in the thick of the action. If the boys in red and white are to succeed then Robert must perform.

Drazen Ladic

Unpredictable goalkeeper but generally solid for Croatia over the years. Looks certain to start in the first team.

Marijan Mrmic

Another erratic goalkeeper who is liable either to save or lose you a game in an instant. Reserve number one.

Robert Jarni

Ferociously quick wing-back who is comfortable in both defensive and attacking positions.

Igor Stimac

Another of the English contingent in the squad. At Derby County he has become a cult figure and has never let the Croatian fans down. Stylish centre-back.

Nicola Jerkan

Since his unsuccessful stint in the English game he has not regained the form that saw so many teams chasing him after the European Championships.

Zvonimir Soldo

Talented attacking player who has rarely broken through into the first team but could be given a chance in France.

Aljosa Asanovic

His ability has never been in question but his commitment to the team has been under scrutiny. It is a shame that there are doubts cast over him because he is able to play some breathtaking football.

Dario Simic

Up-and-coming, versatile player who has been looked at by many of the top sides in Europe. He will hope to impress a top side during the finals.

Nikola Jurcevic

Midfield player who likes to play on the right but has been used in the middle. Comfortable on the ball but not a matchwinner.

Silvio Maric

Another young player who at 22 could prove to be one of the stars of the Croatian team. May be too inexperienced to start.

Igor Cvitanovic

Lively striker who, though fourth choice, could be given a chance on the highest stage.

Zvonimir Boban

Chess-playing midfielder whose passes are as precise as his moves on the chess board. Quality midfielder who is very inspirational for his team-mates.

Mario Stanic

Age	Caps	Value
25	13	£3 million

Enigmatic attacking midfielder who, like so many players, blows hot and cold. His international career has been interrupted by injury and by tactical exclusion from the team on occasions.

His club form has been inconsistent but he is a player who is certain to be in the squad. He is very strong on the ball and forces his way past defenders with style.

How they got there

Group 1

Date	Home		Away	Score
24-Apr-96	Greece	vs.	Slovenia	2:0
01-Sep-96	Greece	vs.	Bosnia-Herzegovina	3:0
01-Sep-96	Slovenia	vs.	Denmark	0:2
08-Oct-96	Bosnia-Herzegovina	vs.	Croatia	1:4
09-Oct-96	Denmark	vs.	Greece	2:1
10-Nov-96	Slovenia	vs.	Bosnia-Herzegovina	1:2
10-Nov-96	Croatia	vs.	Greece	1:1
29-Mar-97	Croatia	vs.	Denmark	1:1
02-Apr-97	Bosnia-Herzegovina	vs.	Greece	0:1
02-Apr-97	Croatia	vs.	Slovenia	3:3
30-Apr-97	Denmark	vs.	Slovenia	4:0
30-Apr-97	Greece	vs.	Croatia	0:1
08-Jun-97	Denmark	vs.	Bosnia-Herzegovina	2:0
20-Aug-97	Bosnia-Herzegovina	vs.	Denmark	3:0
06-Sep-97	Croatia	vs.	Bosnia-Herzegovina	3:2
06-Sep-97	Slovenia	vs.	Greece	0:3
10-Sep-97	Denmark	vs.	Croatia	3:1
10-Sep-97	Bosnia-Herzegovina	vs.	Slovenia	1:0
11-Oct-97	Slovenia	vs.	Croatia	1:3
11-Oct-97	Greece	vs.	Denmark	0:0

FINAL STANDINGS

Team	P	W	D	L	F	A	Pts
Denmark	8	5	2	1	14	6	17
Croatia	8	4	3	1	17	12	15
Greece	8	4	2	2	11	4	14
Bosnia-Herzegovina	8	3	0	5	9	14	9
Slovenia	8	0	1	7	5	20	1

World Cup Odds

33/1

DENMARK

What are their chances?

It is remarkable to think that this is Denmark's first World Cup finals appearance for 12 years.

Although they qualified, results towards the end of the qualification stage seemed to show a lack of confidence in the squad. With the majority of the first team playing in different countries around Europe it is a messy set-up, with little stability. However, the Laudrups confirmed that they are the most skilful brothers playing in the world game today. Michael, in particluar proved to his many doubters that he still has all the skill and panache of old.

There are also some promising youngsters who could make names for themselves in France. Ebbe Sand is a prolific goalscorer at club level while Soren Colding and Thomas Gravesen are two defenders who both have enormous potential.

Though they face a tough match against the hosts, games against South Africa and Saudi Arabia should see them through to the second phase.

ONE TO WATCH

Group C

Friday June 12
DENMARK V SAUDI ARABIA

Thursday June 18
DENMARK V SOUTH AFRICA

Wednesday June 24
DENMARK V FRANCE

Brian Laudrup

Age	Caps	Value
28	73	£6 million

Brian will have the spotlight on him after making the move to Chelsea and becoming one of the highest-paid players in world football. Having been outstanding for Glasgow Rangers since day one he has produced the same form for his country.

The Laudrup connection is very much alive in the Danish camp and much will depend on Brian and his brother if Denmark are to succeed. He has exquisite skills and poses many problems for opposing teams.

Mikkel Beck

Age	Caps	Value
24	14	£2.5 million

When going into a major tournament such as the World Cup managers look at which strikers are in hot goalscoring form. Though Mikkel is not playing at the highest level, he is one of the most in-form strikers in the Danish squad.

For a tall man he has a good touch allied to pace and skill and he is turning into a top striker. He has a lot to prove after a disappointing season in the Premiership in 1996-97 and there is no better stage than the World Cup.

Allan Nielsen

Age	Caps	Value
26	14	£1.5 million

The Tottenham midfielder has not been in favour of late for either club or country and could struggle to make the first-team. It is a real dip in fortunes for the Danish midfielder who was voted Danish player of the year a few years ago.

He is a defensive midfielder who ventures forward on occasions and has a knack of getting into some good goalscoring positions.

Profiles of the rest of the squad

Marc Rieper

The former West Ham defender has enjoyed success with Celtic over the past year; and being high on confidence is a superb asset to take into a major tournament. With close to 50 caps he is a rock at the centre of the defence. Though he does not have an impressive scoring record for his country, he notches quite a few goals for his club and can be a real handful at set-pieces.

Jon Dahl Tomasson

Much was expected of Jon Dahl Tomasson in his first season at Newcastle but he has not made great progress. There have been moments of magic and some impressive performances but it seems that he is maybe too young for the big time. In his performances for the national side he has done well and it could be that he performs at the very highest level. He could be the future Michael Laudrup that Denmark so desperately need.

Mogens Krogh

Reserve goalkeeper who has never really had a chance to prove himself, while Schmeichal has commanded the number one jersey..

Jes Hogh

Quality defender who is one of the most experienced in the squad. Very reliable at right-back; solid and strong.

Jacob Laursen

Can play across the back line and has proved at Derby County that he can take on some of the finest strikers in the world.

Thomas Gravesen

A young centre-back with a bright future ahead. Many have tipped him to be the next Beckenbauer. He has the potential, this could be the time to fulfil it.

Bjarne Goldbaek

Extremely skilful midfielder who is often overshadowed by the Laudrups. Comfortable playing in the middle or on either wing; a very influential player for the side.

Morten Wieghorst

In his past few seasons for Celtic he has improved a great deal. Whether playing as a central midfielder or just behind the forwards, he is a very useful player to have in the squad.

Peter Moller

Experienced midfielder who will have to settle for a place on the bench, but will be a more than adequate replacement if called upon.

Per Frandsen

Underrated midfielder who has shone for Bolton Wanderers. His nimble feet and quick thinking have earned him a good reputation and could see him gaining a place in the team at some point.

Thomas Helveg

It is easy to distinguish Thomas from many of the other players in the squad because he has spent so many years in the Italian game. He is vital to the team on the right side of midfield.

Soren Colding

Another young defender who has been given a handful of games prior to the World Cup. He will be out to impress the big clubs.

Ebbe Sand

Much talked-about striker who has been linked with clubs around Europe. A phenomenal scoring record could see him make the starting line-up: a scorching prospect.

Michael Laudrup

At 33 he is one of the oldest in the squad but still, without doubt, one of the most talented. Recent form for Ajax has been very promising and he will hope to bow out of surely his final World Cup with a bang. You have been warned!

DENMARK

Peter Schmeichel

Age	Caps	Value
34	97	£2 million

Peter is still thought of as one of the best goalkeepers in the world and his performances for both club and country support that view. His last-gasp save against Greece in the qualifying stage saw Denmark reach the World Cup. Danish fans have much to thank Peter for.

He may scream and shout at his defenders but that is all part of his character. Extremely agile and astonishingly fit, managers around the world would give anything to have him in their goal.

How they got there

Group 1

Date	Home		Away	Score
24-Apr-96	Greece	vs.	Slovenia	2:0
01-Sep-96	Greece	vs.	Bosnia-Herzegovina	3:0
01-Sep-96	Slovenia	vs.	Denmark	0:2
08-Oct-96	Bosnia-Herzegovina	vs.	Croatia	1:4
09-Oct-96	Denmark	vs.	Greece	2:1
10-Nov-96	Slovenia	vs.	Bosnia-Herzegovina	1:2
10-Nov-96	Croatia	vs.	Greece	1:1
29-Mar-97	Croatia	vs.	Denmark	1:1
02-Apr-97	Bosnia-Herzegovina	vs.	Greece	0:1
02-Apr-97	Croatia	vs.	Slovenia	3:3
30-Apr-97	Denmark	vs.	Slovenia	4:0
30-Apr-97	Greece	vs.	Croatia	0:1
08-Jun-97	Denmark	vs.	Bosnia-Herzegovina	2:0
20-Aug-97	Bosnia-Herzegovina	vs.	Denmark	3:0
06-Sep-97	Croatia	vs.	Bosnia-Herzegovina	3:2
06-Sep-97	Slovenia	vs.	Greece	0:3
10-Sep-97	Denmark	vs.	Croatia	3:1
10-Sep-97	Bosnia-Herzegovina	vs.	Slovenia	1:0
11-Oct-97	Slovenia	vs.	Croatia	1:3
11-Oct-97	Greece	vs.	Denmark	0:0

FINAL STANDINGS

Denmark	8	5	2	1	14	6	17
Croatia	8	4	3	1	17	12	15
Greece	8	4	2	2	11	4	14
Bosnia-Herzegovina	8	3	0	5	9	14	9
Slovenia	8	0	1	7	5	20	1

World Cup Odds

33/1

What are their chances ?

Four years ago the Nigerians produced some of the best football in World Cup '94 in the United States. Since then Nigeria have been outstanding in the Olympic Games where stronger sides like Brazil and Argentina were brushed aside by the emerging Nigerian team - things are looking up for the boys from Africa.

The squad now is stronger than it has ever been with a blend of youth and experience that may bring success. Not only is there a mixture of ages, but there is also many players who display their skills at some of the biggest clubs in Europe. George, Ikpeba, Okocha and Babangida are all gifted players whom many managers now know about and fear.

There are weaknesses in the side though - a defence that lacks concentration during games and a suspect goalkeeper - traits that many African teams have and Nigeria are no different.

There is no doubt they face the hardest task in trying to qualify from their group and it will be a true test of the Nigerians' improvement if they progress to the later stages. The side contains more talent than many of their counterparts, but a lack of strength in depth and organisational abilities will probably see them fail.

ONE TO WATCH

Group D

Saturday June 13 **NIGERIA V SPAIN**
Friday June 19 **NIGERIA V BULGARIA**
Wednesday June 24 **NIGERIA V PARAGUAY**

Finidi George

Age	Caps	Value
27	35	£3 million

An extremely talented footballer who can run past defenders with ease. He has shown that a major move to Real Betis from Ajax a few seasons ago did not disturb his football. The major stage of the World Cup should similarly not intimidate him.

He is lightning quick with a rapid change of pace, while his trickery and skill make him almost impossible to play against. The only doubt about him is a question mark over his consistency.

Celestine Babayaro

Age	Caps	Value
19	6	£4 million

One of the most talented young players in the world, Celestine has shown that he is exactly the player he was rumoured to be. For Chelsea, he displayed that he can play in one of the most competitive leagues, though he has struggled with injury.

He can play either on the left side or through the middle of the defence or midfield, making him a very versatile squad member. He was one of the stars of the Olympic team and hopes to recreate that form.

Victor Ikpeba

Age	Caps	Value
24	14	£7.5 million

In recent years the attacking talent at Monaco has been truly outstanding, and Ikpeba certainly follows in that tradition. He has everything a striker needs: power, skill and cool finishing.

He will be one of the first names on the team sheet after having had another storming season in France. His natural ability will surely shine even more on the World Cup stage - a riveting prospect.

Profiles of the rest of the squad

Christopher Ohen

Many believed that Chris could develop into one of the most powerful forwards in world football. However, he has never really been able to make a name for himself playing for Compostela in the Spanish Primera. He is a handful for defenders and uses his stocky build to his advantage. Though not prolific, he gets very involved and lays on many goals for the attacking midfielders that are in the Nigerian team.

Daniel Amokachi

After never really being given a fair chance for Everton, Daniel is out to prove that he can perform at the highest level. It was four years ago when he made a name for himself and he hopes that he can repeat those USA '94 performances. An awkward striker to play against, Daniel penetrates the defence with deceptive runs; his change of pace and quick acceleration can be devastating. At 24 he still has time to make the big time once again, and the World Cup is a perfect stage for him to show the managers of Europe what they are missing.

Peter Rufai

At 35 Peter could well play his final games for his country. He is still very athletic and a great character.

Austin Egvavoen

With over 50 caps under his belt Austin is obviously a very important member of the squad. A sound defender with a no-nonsense attitude.

Ben Iroha

Another who has experience of playing in the World Cup, Ben is dangerous coming forward with the ball and can play in midfield or attack.

Taribo West

Those who have never seen Taribo in action are sure to get a shock ! Though his colourful hair and wild temper are often the main talking points, he is also a very solid and talented defender.

Nwankwo Kanu

Kanu captained the much talked-about Olympic side that was so successful. The football world holds their breath to see if he can recover from a heart problem and fulfil his potential.

Sunday Oliseh

The linchpin in the centre of the midfield, he adds some steel to the flair that surrounds him. Well travelled and full of experience, Sunday is a very important player to the side.

Jay-Jay Okocha

On his day one of the most attractive players to watch in the footballing world. He is strong but possesses very quick feet. Many of Nigeria's attacking ideas come from Jay-Jay.

Tijani Babangida

Though he may not get a starting place, Tiji is a player who has the ability to change a game. His time at Ajax has strengthened his game, while his ability was never in doubt.

Mutiu Adepoju

A hearty midfield player who is widely respected by the Nigerian fans. Very strong and very committed to the team.

Godwin Okpara

A reserve midfield/attacking player who can do a competent job, though he has little experience and may have to wait for his chance.

Uche Okechukwu

Tall and strong, Uche plays in the heart of the defence. He reads the game well and has skill when moving forward.

Uche Okafor

Okafor either plays in the sweeper role or on the right side of the defence. Determined to show that he can play at the highest level after being dropped.

How they got there

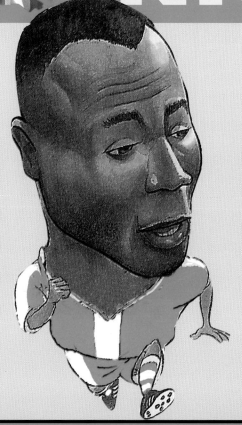

Emmanuel Amunike

Age	Caps	Value
26	25	£5 million

With Finidi George on one wing and Emmanuel on the other Nigeria must have one of the most dangerous teams when it comes to wing play and technical ability.

The Barcelona winger has been inconsistent for his club side but has put in some dazzling performances. For his country, he is thought of as one of Nigeria's most important players. He scores and makes goals: a tantalising prospect for the World Cup.

Group 1

06-Nov-96	Nigeria	vs.	Burkina Fasa	2-0
10-Nov-96	Guinea	vs.	Kenya	3-1
12-Jan-97	Kenya	vs.	Nigeria	1-1
12-Jan-97	Burkina Fasa	vs.	Guinea	0-2
05-Apr-97	Nigeria	vs.	Guinea	2-1
27-Apr-97	Burkina Fasa	vs.	Nigeria	1-2
27-Apr-97	Kenya	vs.	Guinea	1-0
07-Jun-97	Nigeria	vs.	Kenya	3-0
08-Jun-97	Guinea	vs.	Burkina Fasa	3-1
17-Aug-97	Guinea	vs.	Nigeria	1-0
17-Aug-97	Burkina Fasa	vs.	Kenya	2-4

FINAL STANDINGS

Nigeria	6	4	1	1	10	4	13
Guinea	6	4	0	2	10	5	12
Kenya	6	3	1	2	11	12	10
Burkina Fasa	6	0	0	6	7	17	0

World Cup Odds

25/1

What are their chances ?

Qualification was a breeze and though they are probably the most unfashionable team going to France they are surely one of the most effective. The coach, Egil Olsen, will retire once his team has finished their World Cup campaign and whether he wins the trophy or loses all three of his group games he will go down as the greatest ever Norwegian manager. He is idolised in his country and is a national hero.

The squad includes many players who ply their trade in the English Premiership. Though they are not all the most talented of footballers, and are not full of flamboyance or trickery, they work tremendously hard as a unit. They also have the added bonus of seeing each other regularly - training sessions are held in England.

There is a strong spine in the team: Johnsen and Berg at the back, Leonhardsen and Haaland through the midfield with Solskjaer and probably Flo filling the striker's role. All solid players who have developed their skills in the Premiership.

A group containing the holders, Brazil, and Scotland sees them face a difficult route to the second phase, and a lack of flair players may well see them miss out.

ONE TO WATCH

Group A

Wednesday June 10	
NORWAY V MORROCO	
Tuesday June 16	
NORWAY V SCOTLAND	
Tuesday June 23	
NORWAY V BRAZIL	

Ole Gunnar Solskjaer

Age	Caps	Value
24	10	£8 million

When Alex Ferguson brought in Solskjaer from Norwegian club Molde for £1.5 million many questioned his judgement. Now he is worth at least four times that and goes to France hoping to live up to his ever-growing reputation.

His small frame and slim body are extremely deceptive; he can hold the ball up and has the power to turn defenders. He is deadly in front of goal and the 'baby-faced assassin' will take any chance he gets.

Oyvind Leonhardsen

Age	Caps	Value
27	53	£5 million

Much of the Norwegian squad plays in the English Premiership but no-one has improved his game more than Oyvind Leonhardsen. Now playing for Liverpool, his confidence is riding high.

Oyvind is a busy player who is always right in the thick of the action. He is preferred in a more central position for his country, where he is allowed the freedom to dictate the game.

Ronny Johnsen

Age	Caps	Value
28	31	£4 million

A composed defender who can also play in midfield. Though he has suffered form injury in the last season, if he is fit enough to play he will be a great asset to the team.

He is strong and has a touch of class; he has been referred to as a 'Brazilian in disguise' on occasion. Such comments may flatter him, but he is a very competent defender.

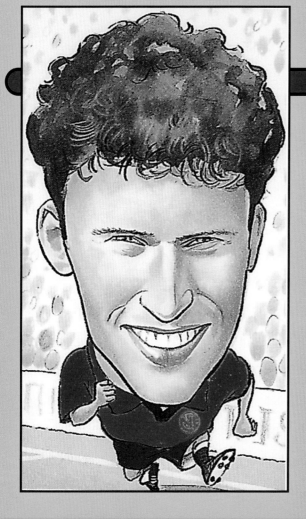

Profiles of the rest of the squad

Alfe-Inge Haaland

Another who has improved his game during his time in the Premiership, Alfe Inge is the cog in the Norwegian midfield. He is the linkman, playing as anchor in front of the back four. After a slow start to his career with Leeds he eventually began to impress the fans with his determination and tenacious football. Though he does play in a defensive role, he often gets forward and has an impressive goalscoring record for a defensive midfielder.

Stig-Inge Bjornebye

Though Stig is no longer an automatic choice for the Liverpool side, his place in the national side has been very stable. He has not let his topsy-turvy domestic career affect his form for Norway. Stig is a superb crosser of the ball, strikers who play with him will say how precise he is with his centres into the box. It will be likely that he will play on the left side of the midfield, allowing him to get forward more.

Frode Grodas

Veteran goalkeeper who showed at his time at Chelsea that he is an athlete and can pull off the most magnificent saves or let in the most simple goals.

Henning Berg

Tremendously fit, 'world-class' defender whose move to Manchester United seems to have improved his game.

Gunnar Halle

Another veteran who is not likely to make the starting line-up. After spending many years at lowly Oldham he recently moved to Leeds.

Roger Nilson

Steely defender who makes up for his lack of technical skill with his solidity in the heart of the defence.

Lars Bohinen

Lars has been out of favour for Blackburn Rovers but still has an important role to play as the main attacking midfiedler for the Norwegian team.

Stale Solbakken

Solbakken is another of the Norwegian squad who plays in England. Defensive midfielder who passes the ball very accurately.

Petter Rudi

The Sheffield Wednesday midfielder has become a firm favourite with the crowd in his first season. A very intelligent footballer.

Tore Andre Flo

Strong and deceptively quick, he is the striker that Norway have needed for a long time.

Egil Ostenstad

Another attacking option for the side. He would have been regarded as a first-team player but long injury lay-offs will probably see him start on the bench.

Kjetl Rekdal

Veteran midfield player who is one of the few squad mambers not to be playing in England. Very experienced and inspirational on and off the pitch.

Tore Pedersen

Vastly experienced defender who, though not really having had a chance to show what he can do at Blackburn is a quality player.

How they got there

Group 3				
02-Jun-96	Norway	vs.	Azerbaijan	5:0
31-Aug-96	Azerbaijan	vs.	Switzerland	1:0
01-Sep-96	Hungary	vs.	Finland	1:0
06-Oct-96	Finland	vs.	Switzerland	2:3
09-Oct-96	Norway	vs.	Hungary	3:0
10-Nov-96	Switzerland	vs.	Norway	0:1
10-Nov-96	Azerbaijan	vs.	Hungary	0:3
02-Apr-97	Azerbaijan	vs.	Finland	1:2
30-Apr-97	Norway	vs.	Finland	1:1
30-Apr-97	Switzerland	vs.	Hungary	1:0
08-Jun-97	Finland	vs.	Azerbaijan	3:0
08-Jun-97	Hungary	vs.	Norway	1:1
20-Aug-97	Hungary	vs.	Switzerland	1:1
20-Aug-97	Finland	vs.	Norway	0:4
06-Sep-97	Azerbaijan	vs.	Norway	0:1
06-Sep-97	Switzerland	vs.	Finland	1:2
10-Sep-97	Hungary	vs.	Azerbaijan	3:1
10-Sep-97	Norway	vs.	Switzerland	5:0
11-Sep-97	Finland	vs.	Hungary	1:1
11-Oct-97	Switzerland	vs.	Azerbaijan	5:0

Bjorn Kvarme

Age	Caps	Value
25	0	£3 million

Managers in the Premiership have taken advantage of getting players for bargain prices from Scandinavia. Kvarme is a player who came with absolutely no reputation and is now thought of as one of the most complete defenders in the English game.

He is quick, strong and an excellent tackler. He is a total novice to the national team but if he can display the flexiblity he did with Liverpool then he will be more than comfortable.

FINAL STANDINGS

Norway	8	6	2	0	21	2	20
Hungary	8	3	3	2	10	8	12
Finland	8	3	2	3	11	12	11
Switzerland	8	3	1	4	11	12	10
Azerbaijan	8	1	0	7	3	22	3

World Cup Odds

50/1

ROMANIA

What are their chances ?

Romania had the prestige of being one of the top eight seeds. Though many were surprised, they were extremely impressive in the qualification rounds, having a 100 per cent record until their final game.

Many criticised the coach, Angel Iordanescu, after a very disappointing Euro '96 campaign, but he has come back with a vengeance. Though many called for changes in the side, he decided to stick with his formula and his wise tactics have seen his team become one of the strongest forces in Europe.

A group which sees them face England and Colombia cannot be too comforting for Romania, but as they showed in America four years ago, they like to play as underdogs. They proved to be one of the greatest successes in world football when they reached the quarter-finals in America but it will be hard to repeat such performances.

Hagi is still the danger man, though opposing teams have had enough time to figure a game plan to counteract him. Adrian Illie is an exciting striker and there is an abundance of ability in the squad: Petrescu, Moldovan, Muteanu and Dumitrescu. One problem lies in the lack of a fresh faces, the squad is pretty much the same as it was four years ago. A second-phase place, but no more.

ONE TO WATCH

Group G

Monday June 15 ROMANIA V COLOMBIA
Monday June 22 ROMANIA V ENGLAND
Friday June 26 ROMANIA V TUNISIA

Illie Dumitrescu

Age	Caps	Value
28	60	£4 million

Since the World Cup finals in America Illie's career has seen many ups and downs. Initially his move to Tottenham Hotspur looked to be a success but after a string of injuries and then a fruitless spell at West Ham he saw himself completely out of the picture, both domestically and on the international scene.

He has had recent success in Mexico and Spain and has started to work his way back into the national set-up. He is a very talented player who can play anywhere across the midfield or in a striker's role.

Dan Petrescu

Age	Caps	Value
30	64	£3 million

Extremely talented player who has shown at Chelsea that he has much more ability than first thought when he arrived in the English game. He was initially bought as a full-back but has displayed such fine attacking qualities that he is now preferred in a midfield role.

He is very quick and likes to get involved all the time. His passing is good and he has a tendency to pop up with some spectacular goals.

Tibor Selymes

Age	Caps	Value
27	42	£2 million

One of the Romanian contingent who earns his living in the German game, he is a player who likes to orchestrate the midfield with good movement and accurate passing.

He is a pacy player with quick feet and an intelligent footballing brain. He has proved that he can compete at the top level of the game for both club and country and will play an important role in the underrated Romanian team.

Profiles of the rest of the squad

Florin Prunea

Flamboyant goalkeeper who is never guaranteed a place in the team due to some awful performances. Brilliant or terrible depending on what mood he is in.

Bogdon Stelea

Stelea has battled with Prunea for the number one spot and though he may not be as agile as his colleague he seems a safer bet in goal and will probably start the tournament.

Anton Dobos

Defender in form, looked at by many of the top clubs in Europe, he is hoping he can perform to his highest level in France.

Iulina Filipescu

Up-and-coming defensive midfielder being groomed to take over the position of Georghe Popescu; impressive in the qualification rounds.

Daniel Prodan

Strong and very reliable, he is a vital player to the Romanians and will be a rock at the heart of the defence.

Ion Lupescu

Versatile midfielder who is very steady in the middle of the park. Do not expect anything too spectacular from him, he does a lot of important work that is never applauded.

Dorinel Muteanu

Strong in the midfield has played away from his home country, giving him an insight into some of his opponents. Likes to orchestrate the midfield.

Ovidiu Stinga

Reserve attacking midfielder; has shown he has a lot of ability but is unlikely to feature in the starting line-up.

Adrian Illie

Young striker who is now coming into his prime. Illie has a real eye for goal and was very impressive in the qualification rounds.

Catalin Munteanu

Precocious youngster who has displayed some quite outstanding football for Steau Bucharest in the last few seasons.

Florin Raduciou

There is no-one who would like to show the world what he can do more than Raduciou. After being one of the stars of America he has faded from the football world; so much to prove.

George Hagi

The World Cup would not be the same without watching the delightful George Hagi. Now playing in his fourth World Cup finals, Hagi looks almost certain to bow out of international football when Romania finish their campaign in France. He lacks the fitness that he once had but his skills and vision are still to be wondered at. Romania's finest ever player is still their key to success. If he performs the team thrives .

Marius Lacatus

It was in the World Cup of '86 when Marius came onto the scene and was hailed one of the most exciting players in Europe. Though he has never seemed to make the greatest of impacts, since then he has been a great servant to the national team. He may not feature in the first team but will be important to the squad both on and off the pitch. He could well be retiring from international football after the World Cup but don't be surprised to see him at the helm of the national team in the future.

Viorel Moldovan

His recent move to the Premiership did not see him make the kind of impact he would have liked, but he has shown that he is a quality player. A multi-million-pound move saw Viorel join Coventry and he is sure to be a welcome addition to the English game. Though not the tallest of players, he uses his stocky frame to bustle past defenders. He is very tricky on the ball and is a decent finisher.

How they got there

Group 9

Date	Home		Away	Score
24-Apr-96	FYR Macedonia	vs.	Liechtenstein	3:0
01-Jun-96	Iceland	vs.	FYR Macedonia	1:1
31-Aug-96	Liechtenstein	vs.	Republic of Ireland	0:5
31-Aug-96	Romania	vs.	Lithuania	3:0
05-Oct-96	Lithuania	vs.	Iceland	2:0
09-Oct-96	Lithuania	vs.	Liechtenstein	2:1
09-Oct-96	Iceland	vs.	Romania	0:4
09-Oct-96	Republic of Ireland	vs.	FYR Macedonia	3:0
09-Nov-96	Liechtenstein	vs.	FYR Macedonia	1:11
10-Nov-96	Republic of Ireland	vs.	Iceland	0:0
14-Dec-96	FYR Macedonia	vs.	Romania	0:3
29-Mar-97	Romania	vs.	Liechtenstein	8:0
02-Apr-97	FYR Macedonia	vs.	Republic of Ireland	3:2
02-Apr-97	Lithuania	vs.	Romania	0:1
30-Apr-97	Liechtenstein	vs.	Lithuania	0:2
30-Apr-97	Romania	vs.	Republic of Ireland	1:0
21-May-97	Republic of Ireland	vs.	Liechtenstein	5:0
07-Jun-97	FYR Macedonia	vs.	Iceland	1:0
11-Jun-97	Iceland	vs.	Lithuania	0:0
20-Aug-97	Liechtenstein	vs.	Iceland	0:4
20-Aug-97	Republic of Ireland	vs.	Lithuania	0:0
20-Aug-97	Romania	vs.	FYR Macedonia	4:2
06-Sep-97	Iceland	vs.	Republic of Ireland	2:4
06-Sep-97	Liechtenstein	vs.	Romania	1:8
06-Sep-97	Lithuania	vs.	FYR Macedonia	2:0
10-Sep-97	Romania	vs.	Iceland	4:0
10-Sep-97	Lithuania	vs.	Republic of Ireland	1:2
11-Oct-97	Iceland	vs.	Liechtenstein	4:0
11-Oct-97	Republic of Ireland	vs.	Romania	1:1
11-Oct-97	FYR Macedonia	vs.	Lithuania	1:2

Georghe Popescu

Age	Caps	Value
30	74	£2 million

Another of the Romanian squad who made a name for himself in previous World Cups. Though he has not been playing as regularly as he was at the time of the World Cup four years ago, he is still a very composed and cool-headed player on the ball.

Georghe prefers to play in midfield but is often brought back into the defence where he is a match for some of the greatest strikers in the world. Having played for Barcelona and Tottenham Hotspur, he has wide experience.

FINAL STANDINGS

Team							
Romania	10	9	1	0	37	4	28
Rep. of Ireland	10	5	3	2	22	8	18
Lithuania	10	5	2	3	11	8	17
FYR Macedonia	10	4	1	5	22	18	13
Iceland	10	2	3	5	11	16	9
Liechtenstein	10	0	0	10	3	52	0

World Cup Odds

25/1

What are their chances ?

When being reinstated into the football world in 1994 many underestimated the Yugoslavians. Under the management of Slobodon Santec they have surprised many with their slick football which at times has been close to brilliant.

They were unfortunate not to gain automatic qualification but made up for it when destroying Hungary in the play-off. There have been questions over whether they are able to rise to the big occasion; they never troubled Spain in their qualification group, away or in Belgrade.

There is great buoyancy in the side; with this spirit and the amount of ability in the squad they are bound to turn a few heads. Yugoslavia are a very attack-minded team and players such as Mijatovic, Savicevic, Pantic and Milosovic are among the most talented footballers in the world.

Many around the world are starting to take their challenge seriously. Santec would have liked to have taken his side into the tournament as dark horses but it now looks as though they are expected to do well, pressure that surely isn't welcome. A quarter final place is likely.

ONE TO WATCH

Group F

Sunday June 14
YUGOSLAVIA V IRAN

Sunday June 21
YUGOSLAVIA V GERMANY

Thursday June 25
YUGOSLAVIA V U.S.A.

Dejan Savicevic

Age	Caps	Value
31	48	£6 million

In Savicevic and Mijatovic Yugoslavia have possibly the most dangerous strike force in France. Both players blow hot and cold and it really does depend on what mood they are in, but they have the ability to produce some magic moments.

Dejan is still regarded as one of the top strikers in the Italian Serie A. He has an abundance of skill and has been classed in the same league as Pele on occasions - there is no greater compliment.

Dragan Stojkovic

Age	Caps	Value
32	61	£1 million

A midfielder who, on his day, is as good as anyone. He is one of the most experienced players in the squad and is going to be extremely important to the team who will look to him for inspiration.

He can play in a wide position or through the middle, either way he is extremely effective. He is one of the few Yugoslav players with experience in a major tournament, and that will count for a lot when they go to France.

Vladamir Jugovic

Age	Caps	Value
28	20	£3 million

Another player who many believe could be one of the key members of the Yugoslavian squad. For years he has played some of the best football of his career in Serie A and has now recreated that form for his country.

Jugovic could prove to be one of the most electric midfielders in France. With him and Pantic at the heart of the team everything is there: tackling, passing, goals and 100 per cent effort.

Profiles of the rest of the squad

Savo Milosovic

Recent events on and off the pitch have seen Savo in the headlines for the wrong reasons. He is hoping that by June he can put everything behind him and let his football do the talking. In spite of his troubles his game has improved and he is now starting to show the quality that was so often talked about. He has a delicate touch for a big man and likes to shoot from the most audacious positions.

Milinko Pantic

For reasons unknown, Milinko was not selected for much of the World Cup qualifying campaign. It looks as though he may be given his chance in France though; he has demonstrated over the past few years that he is one of the most complete midfielders in the game. Always playing in the heart of the Athletico Madrid midfield he seems to be involved, whether tracking back to help the defence or getting forward to score goals.

Aleksander Kocic

Aleksander will battle with his rivals for the number one jersey. He is tall and commanding, though has a tendency to let his mind wander.

Drago Lekovic

The former Kilmarnock goalkeeper has not been in the best of form lately for Sporting Gijon and may well have to settle for a place on the bench.

Zoran Mirkovic

Reliable defender whose experience will be very important to the side. He looked an extremely competent defender in the qualifying rounds.

Albert Nadj

Very strong defender who gets little recognition as much of the attention is centred on some of the more attacking players. Will impress many.

Branco Brnovic

He will be fighting for one of the midfield places. An apparent increase in commitment has added much to his game and he has a lot of ability, but like many of his compatriots, he needs to be in the mood.

Slavisa Jokanovic

Exciting midfield/forward player who could be a real matchwinner for the side.

Zeljko Petrovic

Yet another midfield player who has earned over 10 caps. He is likely to start on the bench but his tenacious qualities could well be called upon.

Ljublinko Drulovic

Having played in Portugal for the majority of his career, he has a wealth of experience and can read the game very well.

Dragan Ciric

Exciting striker who has made progress during his spell with Barcelona. He has a lot of talent but will have to wait for his chance.

Darko Kovacevic

After an unsuccessful spell with Sheffield Wednesday he has been a huge hit in Spain and is fiercely challenging for a place in the side.

Dejan Stefanovic

Though not impressing at Sheffield Wednesday he still is firmly in the plans of Santec and will relish every moment of the World Cup.

Pedrag Mijatovic

Undoubtedly one of the finest talents on show in France. For Real Madrid he has been in sizzling form; he spells danger to all defences that have to face him.

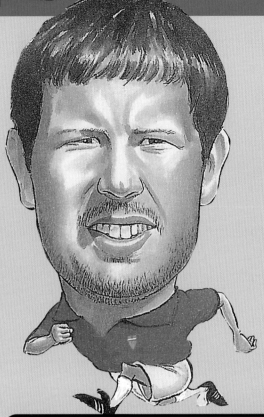

Sinisa Mihailovic

Age	Caps	Value
28	26	£3.5 million

It is no coincidence that the rise of Yugoslavian football has coincided with the remarkable form of Mihailovic. He has been one of the most consistent players for both Sampdoria and Yugoslavia over the past three years.

Though he is mainly a defensive player who is more comfortable with his left foot, he is feared throughout the game from set-pieces. There are very few players who can hit the target so accurately from free-kicks.

How they got there

Group 1

24-Apr-96	Yugoslavia	vs.	Faroe Islands	3:1
02-Jun-96	Yugoslavia	vs.	Malta	6:0
31-Aug-96	Faroe Islands	vs.	Slovakia	1:2
04-Sep-96	Faroe Islands	vs.	Spain	2:6
18-Sep-96	Czech Republic	vs.	Malta	6:0
22-Sep-96	Slovakia	vs.	Malta	6:0
06-Oct-96	Faroe Islands	vs.	Yugoslavia	1:8
09-Oct-96	Czech Republic	vs.	Spain	0:0
23-Oct-96	Slovakia	vs.	FaroeIslands	3:0
10-Nov-96	Yugoslavia	vs.	Czech Republic	1:0
13-Nov-96	Spain	vs.	Slovakia	4:1
14-Dec-96	Spain	vs.	Yugoslavia	2:0
18-Dec-96	Malta	vs.	Spain	0:3
12-Feb-97	Spain	vs.	Malta	4:0
31-Mar-97	Malta	vs.	Slovakia	0:2
02-Apr-97	Czech Republic	vs.	Yugoslavia	1:2
30-Apr-97	Malta	vs.	Faroe Islands	1:2
30-Apr-97	Yugoslavia	vs.	Spain	1:1
08-Jun-97	Faroe Islands	vs.	Malta	2:1
08-Jun-97	Yugoslavia	vs.	Slovakia	2:0
08-Jun-97	Spain	vs.	Czech Republic	1:0
20-Aug-97	Czech Republic	vs.	Faroe Islands	2:0
24-Aug-97	Slovakia	vs.	Czech Republic	2:1
06-Sep-97	Faroe Islands	vs.	Czech Republic	0:2
10-Sep-97	Slovakia	vs.	Yugoslavia	1:1
24-Sep-97	Malta	vs.	Czech Republic	0:1
24-Sep-97	Slovakia	vs.	Spain	1:2
11-Oct-97	Malta	vs.	Yugoslavia	0:5
11-Oct-97	Spain	vs.	Faroe Islands	3:1
11-Oct-97	Czech Republic	vs.	Slovakia	3:0

FINAL STANDINGS

Spain	10	8	2	0	26	6	26
Yugoslavia	10	7	2	1	29	7	23
Czech Rep	10	5	1	4	16	6	16
Slovakia	10	5	1	4	18	14	16
Faroe Islands	10	2	0	8	10	31	6
Malta	10	0	0	10	2	37	0

World Cup Odds

18/1

AUSTRIA

Heimo Pfeifenberger

Age	Caps	Value
24	20	£4 million

Buzzing midfielder playing right in the heart of the midfield. Much has been said about Heimo who has made a real name for himself in the German Bundesliga.

Werder Breman have benefited from his intelligent passing and non-stop running. Forever making chances and creating for others, he doesn't often get forward to score goals.

Group B

Thursday June 11
AUSTRIA V CAMEROON

Wednesday June 17
AUSTRIA V CHILE

Tuesday June 23
AUSTRIA V ITALY

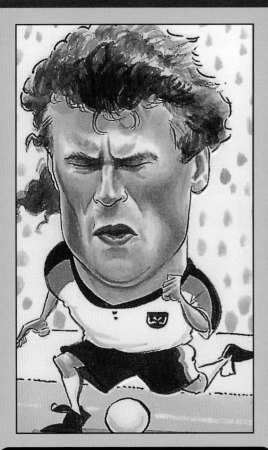

Anton Polster

Age	Caps	Value
33	89	£2 million

Anton is a national hero in Austria. Over the years he has demonstrated leadership on the pitch and it is obvious that he feels it is a genuine honour to represent his country.

Having played in the Bundesliga for the majority of his career, he has been around some of the top players in the world. He is strong and very experienced, giving him an edge over many defenders.

FINAL STANDINGS

How they got there

Group 4

Date	Home		Away	Score
01-Jun-96	Sweden	vs.	Belarus	5:1
31-Aug-96	Belarus	vs.	Estonia	1:0
31-Aug-96	Austria	vs.	Scotland	0:0
01-Sep-96	Latvia	vs.	Sweden	1:2
05-Oct-96	Estonia	vs.	Belarus	1:0
05-Oct-96	Latvia	vs.	Scotland	0:2
09-Oct-96	Belarus	vs.	Latvia	1:1
09-Oct-96	Sweden	vs.	Austria	0:1
09-Nov-96	Austria	vs.	Latvia	2:1
10-Nov-96	Scotland	vs.	Sweden	1:0
11-Feb-97	Estonia	vs.	Scotland	0:0
29-Mar-97	Scotland	vs.	Estonia	2:0
02-Apr-97	Scotland	vs.	Austria	2:0
30-Apr-97	Latvia	vs.	Belarus	2:0
30-Apr-97	Sweden	vs.	Scotland	2:1
30-Apr-97	Austria	vs.	Estonia	2:0
18-May-97	Estonia	vs.	Latvia	1:3
08-Jun-97	Belarus	vs.	Scotland	0:1
08-Jun-97	Latvia	vs.	Austria	1:3
08-Jun-97	Estonia	vs.	Sweden	2:3
20-Aug-97	Estonia	vs.	Austria	0:3
20-Aug-97	Belarus	vs.	Sweden	1:2
06-Sep-97	Latvia	vs.	Estonia	1:0
06-Sep-97	Austria	vs.	Sweden	1:0
07-Sep-97	Scotland	vs.	Belarus	4:1
10-Sep-97	Sweden	vs.	Latvia	1:0
10-Sep-97	Belarus	vs.	Austria	0:1
11-Oct-97	Scotland	vs.	Latvia	2:0
11-Oct-97	Austria	vs.	Belarus	4:0
11-Oct-97	Sweden	vs.	Estonia	1:0

Team	P	W	D	L	F	A	Pts
Austria	10	8	1	1	17	4	25
Scotland	10	7	2	1	15	3	23
Sweden	10	7	0	3	16	9	21
Latvia	10	3	1	6	10	14	10
Estonia	10	1	1	8	4	16	4
Belarus	10	1	1	8	5	21	4

World Cup Odds

80/1

Enzo Scifo

Age	Caps	Value
31	79	£2.5 million

When fit, Scifo is the brains of the Belgium team. However, he has suffered from niggling injuries over the past few years - but he still has the talent that had the whole of the football world chasing him at one point.

There is talent in the Belgium squad and they never seem to have been rewarded for some decent enough performances against the big teams. There could be a lack of confidence in the side that often does look unconvincing.

Group E

Saturday June 13
BELGIUM V HOLLAND

Saturday June 20
BELGIUM V MEXICO

Thursday June 25
BELGIUM V SOUTH KOREA

Luc Nilis

Age	Caps	Value
30	43	£ 4 million

Highly respected striker in the European game, he has been the driving force behind the success of Dutch side PSV Eindhoven over the past few years.

Unfortunately for Luc he does not have the same quality surrounding him and he will struggle to find the net as constantly as he does for his club as a lone striker. Unquestionable talent who can score some outstanding goals.

How they got there

Group 7

Date	Home		Away	Score
02-Jun-96	San Marino	vs.	Wales	0:5
31-Aug-96	Wales	vs.	San Marino	6:0
31-Aug-96	Belgium	vs.	Turkey	2:1
05-Oct-96	Wales	vs.	Holland	1:3
09-Oct-96	San Marino	vs.	Belgium	0:3
09-Nov-96	Holland	vs.	Wales	7:1
10-Nov-96	Turkey	vs.	San Marino	7:0
14-Dec-96	Wales	vs.	Turkey	0:0
14-Dec-96	Belgium	vs.	Holland	0:3
29-Mar-97	Wales	vs.	Belgium	1:2
29-Mar-97	Holland	vs.	San Marino	4:0
02-Apr-97	Turkey	vs.	Holland	1:0
30-Apr-97	Turkey	vs.	Belgium	1:3
30-Apr-97	San Marino	vs.	Holland	0:6
07-Jun-97	Belgium	vs.	San Marino	6:0
20-Aug-97	Turkey	vs.	Wales	6:4
06-Sep-97	Holland	vs.	Belgium	3:1
10-Sep-97	San Marino	vs.	Turkey	0:5
11-Oct-97	Belgium	vs.	Wales	3:2
11-Oct-97	Holland	vs.	Turkey	0:0

FINAL STANDINGS

Holland	8	6	1	1	26	4	19
Belgium	8	6	0	2	20	11	18
Turkey	8	4	2	2	21	9	14
Wales	8	2	1	5	20	21	7
San Marino	8	0	0	8	0	42	0

Belgium beat Republic of Ireland to qualify

World Cup Odds

50/1

Patrick Mboma

Age	Caps	Value
27	12	£3.5 million

Cameroon's highest profile player, Patrick Mboma has urged many of the top clubs in Europe to watch him as he tries to make a name for himself on the highest stage.

Scoring five goals in the qualifying rounds and being a prolific goalscorer for Gambo Osaka in Japan, he is a player whom many are excited to watch. Big and powerful in the air, he has the ability to cause problems for defences. Cameroon's main threat.

Group B

Thursday June 11
CAMEROON V AUSTRIA

Wednesday June 17
CAMEROON V ITALY

Tuesday June 23
CAMEROON V CHILE

CAMEROON

Jacques Songo'o

Age	Caps	Value
35	70	£1 million

Another player who earns his living at Deportivo he is well admired throughout the game. At the age of 35 he could be one of the oldest players in the World Cup but is still able to perform at the highest level.

Agile goalkeeper who is very experienced at all levels of the game, there has never been any doubting his ability. Cameroon will need his cool head when they face the Italians and Chile.

How they got there

Africa 2nd Qualifying Round - Group 4

Date	Home		Away	Score
10-Nov-96	Angola	vs.	Zimbabwe	2-1
10-Nov-96	Togo	vs.	Cameroon	2-4
12-Jan-97	Cameroon	vs.	Angola	0-0
12-Jan-97	Zimbabwe	vs.	Togo	3-0
06-Apr-97	Angola	vs.	Togo	3-1
06-Apr-97	Cameroon	vs.	Zimbabwe	1-0
27-Apr-97	Zimbabwe	vs.	Angola	0-0
27-Apr-97	Cameroon	vs.	Togo	2-0
08-Jun-97	Angola	vs.	Cameroon	1-1
08-Jun-97	Togo	vs.	Zimbabwe	2-1
17-Aug-97	Togo	vs.	Angola	1-1
17-Aug-97	Zimbabwe	vs.	Cameroon	1-2

FINAL STANDINGS

Cameroon	6	4	2	0	10	4	14
Angola	6	2	4	0	7	4	10
Zimbabwe	6	1	1	4	6	7	4
Togo	6	1	1	4	6	14	4

Cameroon Qualify for finals

World Cup Odds

150/1

Marcelo Salas

Age	Caps	Value
22	32	£14 million

Tipped to be one of the stars of the tournament, he has shown in the qualifying and warm-up games that he is an outstanding talent and can score some absolutely astonishing goals.

Recently purchased by Lazio in a deal worth over £10 million, he is a striker who was thought to be going in to the English game. The Premiership's loss is Serie A's gain and this robust and fantastically skilful player will show that in the World Cup.

Group B

Thursday June 11
CHILE V ITALY

Wednesday June 17
CHILE V AUSTRIA

Tuesday June 23
CHILE V CAMEROON

How they got there

Ivan Zamorano

Age	Caps	Value
30	37	£ 4 million

Though the arrival of Salas on the international scene has taken most of the headlines in Chile, Ivan Zamorano is still a striker to be feared. He has suffered from injury in the past year but would have been Ronaldo's striking partner at Inter if he had been fit.

Playing in Italy and in the top Primera in Spain with Real Madrid, he has obviously aided his all-round game but he, like Salas, is a naturally gifted player. He is ravishing in front of goal and opposing defences should watch out for what could be one of the hottest strikeforces in France.

Chilean Results

Date	Home		Away	Score
02-Jun-96	Venezuela	vs.	Chile	1:1
07-Jul-96	Chile	vs.	Equador	4:1
01-Sep-96	Columbia	vs.	Chile	4:1
09-Oct-96	Paraguay	vs.	Chile	2:1
12-Nov-96	Chile	vs.	Uraguay	1:0
15-Dec-96	Argentina	vs.	Chile	1:1
12-Jan-97	Peru	vs.	Chile	2:1
12-Feb-97	Bolivia	vs.	Chile	1:1
30-Apr-97	Chile	vs.	Venezuela	6:0
08-Jun-97	Equador	vs.	Chile	1:1
06-Jul-97	Chile	vs.	Columbia	4:1
20-Jul-97	Chile	vs.	Paraguay	2:1
20-Aug-97	Uraguay	vs.	Chile	1:0
10-Sep-97	Chile	vs.	Argentina	1:2
12-Sep-97	Chile	vs.	Peru	4:0
16-Nov-97	Chile	vs.	Bolivia	3:0

FINAL STANDINGS

SOUTH AMERICA - ROUND ROBIN QUALIFIERS

Team							
Argentina	16	8	6	2	23	13	30
Paraguay	16	9	2	5	21	14	29
Colombia	16	8	4	4	23	15	28
Chile	16	7	4	5	32	18	25

Top 4 teams qualified

World Cup Odds

100/1

Faustino Asprilla

Age	Caps	Value
28	37	£8 million

A sparkling striker who is bound to give the English defence many headaches when they play each other. Having played at Newcastle for a season and a half and now playing his football at Parma, he has good experience of different formations and styles of play.

A special player with elastic legs, he can produce some breathtaking football on occasions. His main weakness is an inability to be consistent throughout a whole season and with a strenuous tournament like the World Cup he could go missing in one of the games.

Group G

Monday June 15
ROMANIA V COLOMBIA

Monday June 22
COLOMBIA V TUNISIA

Friday June 26
COLOMBIA V ENGLAND

Freddy Rincon

Age	Caps	Value
31	72	£ 1.5 million

After spells in Italy and Spain Freddy is now playing his football in Brazil where he is quite accustomed to the South American style of play. Though he has never been able to settle at a team he has always been a dangerous player who can be a real matchwinner on his day.

Rincon and Asprilla could potentially be one of the most lethal partnerships in France; it really does depend on what side of bed they get out of!

South American

Date	Home		Away	Score
24-Apr-96	Argentina	vs.	Bolivia	3-1
24-Apr-96	Colombia	vs.	Paraguay	3-1
24-Apr-96	Peru	vs.	Colombia	1-1
02-Jun-96	Equador	vs.	Argentina	2-0
07-Jul-96	Colombia	vs.	Bolivia	3-1
07-Jul-96	Argentina	vs.	Bolivia	3-1
01-Sep-96	Argentina	vs.	Bolivia	3-1
01-Sep-96	Argentina	vs.	Bolivia	3-1
09-Oct-96	Ecuador	vs.	Colombia	0-1
09-Oct-96	Venezuela	vs.	Argentina	2-5
10-Nov-96	Bolivia	vs.	Colombia	2-2
15-Dec-96	Argentina	vs.	Chile	1-1
15-Dec-96	Venezeula	vs.	Colombia	0-2
12-Jan-97	Uruguay	vs.	Argentina	0-0
12-Feb-97	Colombia	vs.	Argentina	0-1
02-Apr-97	Bolivia	vs.	Argentina	0-1
02-Apr-97	Paraguay	vs.	Colombia	2-1
30-Apr-97	Argentina	vs.	Ecuador	2-1
30-Apr-97	Colombia	vs.	Peru	0-1
08-Jun-97	Argentina	vs.	Peru	2-0
08-Jun-97	Uruguay	vs.	Colombia	1-1
06-Jul-97	Chile	vs.	Colombia	4-1
20-Jul-97	Argentina	vs.	Venezuela	2-0
20-Jul-97	Colombia	vs.	Ecuador	1-0
20-Aug-97	Colombia	vs.	Bolivia	3-0
10-Sep-97	Chile	vs.	Argentina	1-2
10-Sep-97	Colombia	vs.	Venezuela	1-0
12-Oct-97	Argentina	vs.	Uruguay	0-0
14-Nov-97	Argentine	vs.	Colombia	1-1

FINAL STANDINGS

SOUTH AMERICA - ROUND ROBIN QUALIFIERS

Argentina	16	8	6	2	23	13	30
Paraguay	16	9	2	5	21	14	29
Colombia	16	8	4	4	23	15	28
Chile	16	7	4	5	32	18	25

Top 4 teams qualified

World Cup Odds

66/1

IRAN

Ali Daei

Age	Caps	Value
29	52	£2 million

A good all-round striker who is one of the few Iranians to be playing abroad with Armenia Bielefield. He is Iran's most famous player, scoring nearly 40 goals in just over 52 appearances.

After 9 goals in the qualifying rounds he was dropped by the manager, until a protest organised by fans on the Internet saw him back in the team.

Group F

Sunday June 14
IRAN V YUGOSLAVIA

Sunday June 21
IRAN V USA

Thursday June 25
IRAN V GERMANY

How they got there

Khodadad Azizi

Age	Caps	Value
27	27	£2.5 million

A real handful for defences, he has shown that he is one of the hottest properties in German football at the moment. One of the stars of the Iranian team who scored the goal in Melbourne that saw the Iranians go through to the World Cup.

His partnership with Daei could upset quite a few teams in France - and do not expect Iran to be the soft touch everyone is expecting them to be.

Asia and Qualifying Round - Group A

Date	Home		Away	Score
13-Sep-97	China PR	vs.	Iran	2-4
14-Sep-97	Saudi Arabia	vs.	Kuwait	2-1
19-Sep-97	Iran	vs.	Saudi Arabia	1-1
19-Sep-97	Qatar	vs.	Kuwait	0-2
26-Sep-97	Kuwait	vs.	Iran	1-1
26-Sep-97	Qatar	vs.	China PR	1-1
03-Oct-97	China PR	vs.	Saudi Arabia	1-0
03-Oct-97	Iran	vs.	Qatar	3-0
10-Oct-97	Kuwait	vs.	China PR	1-2
11-Oct-97	Saudi Arabia	vs.	Qatar	1-0
17-Oct-97	Iran	vs.	China PR	4-1
17-Oct-97	Kuwait	vs.	Saudi Arabia	2-1
24-Oct-97	Kuwait	vs.	Qatar	0-1
24-Oct-97	Saudi Arabia	vs.	Qatar	1-0
31-Oct-97	China PR	vs.	Qatar	2-3
31-Oct-97	Iran	vs.	Qatar	0-0
06-Nov-97	Saudi Arabia	vs.	China PR	1-1
07-Nov-97	Qatar	vs.	Iran	2-0
12-Nov-97	China PR	vs.	Qatar	1-0
12-Nov-97	Qatar	vs.	Saudi Arabia	0-1

FINAL STANDINGS

Team							
Saudi Arabia	8	4	2	2	8	6	14
Iran	8	3	3	2	13	8	12
China PR	8	3	2	3	11	14	11
Qatar	8	3	1	4	7	10	10
Kuwait	8	2	2	4	7	8	8

Iran Qualify for finals by beating Australia in Play-Off

World Cup Odds

500/1

Deon Burton

Age	Caps	Value
21	7	£2.5million

A script writer would have found it hard to have written the story of the Jamaican team, but they are going to France in the biggest football tournament in the World.

Deon Burton, the Jamaican's answer to Ronaldo, is adored by fans and has a great rapport with the crowd. He is a tall and awkward forward who is beginning to be a hit in the Premiership with Derby County.

Group H

Sunday June 14
JAMAICA V CROATIA

Sunday June 21
JAMAICA V ARGENTINA

Friday June 26
JAMAICA V JAPAN

JAMAICA

Robbie Earle

Age	Caps	Value
32	5	£ 1 million

Many of the English players playing in the Premiership have tried to jump on the Jamaican bandwagon, but Robbie Earle was one of the few who recognised the potential and has been a sole survivor throughout the qualification rounds.

A few seasons ago many believed that Robbie had what it took to play for England, but after being shut out he has performed to an outstanding standard for the Reggae Boys. Uncompromising midfielder with a good footballing brain.

How they got there

Concaraf Final qualifying Group

Date	Home		Away	Score
02-Mar-97	Mexico	vs.	Canada	4-0
02-Mar-97	Jamaica	vs.	USA	0-0
16-Mar-97	USA	vs.	Canada	3-0
16-Mar-97	Costa Rica	vs.	Mexico	0-0
23-Mar-97	Costa Rica	vs.	Canada	3-2
06-Apr-97	Canada	vs.	El Salvador	0-0
13-Apr-97	Mexico	vs.	Jamaica	6-0
20-Apr-97	USA	vs.	Mexico	2-2
27-Apr-97	Canada	vs.	Jamaica	0-0
04-May-97	El Salvador	vs.	Costa Rica	2-1
11-May-97	Costa Rica	vs.	Jamaica	3-1
18-Jun-97	Jamaica	vs.	El Salvador	1-0
01-Jun-97	Canada	vs.	Costa Rica	1-0
08-Jun-97	El Salvador	vs.	Mexico	0-1
29-Jun-97	El Salvador	vs.	USA	1-1
10-Aug-97	Costa Rica	vs.	El Salvador	0-0
07-Sep-97	USA	vs.	Costa Rica	1-0
07-Sep-97	Jamaica	vs.	Canada	1-0
14-Sep-97	Jamaica	vs.	Costa Rica	1-0
14-Sep-97	El Salvador	vs.	Canada	4-1
03-Oct-97	USA	vs.	Jamaica	1-1
05-Oct-97	Mexico	vs.	El Salvador	5-0
12-Oct-97	Canada	vs.	Mexico	2-2
02-Nov-97	Mexico	vs.	USA	0-0
09-Nov-97	Canada	vs.	USA	0-3
09-Nov-97	El Salvador	vs.	Jamaica	2-2
09-Nov-97	Mexico	vs.	Costa Rica	3-3
16-Nov-97	Jamaica	vs.	Mexico	0-0
16-Nov-97	Costa Rica	vs.	Canada	3-1
16-Nov-97	USA	vs.	El Salvador	4-2

FINAL STANDINGS

Team	P	W	D	L	F	A	Pts
Mexico	10	4	6	0	23	7	18
USA	10	4	5	1	17	8	17
Jamaica	10	3	5	2	7	12	14
Costa Rica	10	3	3	4	13	12	12
El Salvador	10	2	4	4	11	16	10
Canada	10	1	3	6	5	20	6

Mexico, USA, Jamaica, Costa Rica Qualified for finals

World Cup Odds

250/1

Kazoyushi Miura

Age	Caps	Value
30	85	£1 million

A gifted striker who had spell in Brazil and in Italy with Genoa and is now playing in the ever-improving 'J' League. Strong in the air and very dangerous in front of goal, he gives the Japanese an edge which will be desperately needed when they face Argentina and Croatia.

With very few attacking options he could be asked to play a holding role in the front line, a position he will look at as a challenge.

Group H

Sunday June 14
JAPAN V ARGENTINA

Saturday June 20
JAPAN V CROATIA

Friday June 26
JAPAN V JAMAICA

ONE TO WATCH

Masami Ihara

Age	Caps	Value
30	110	£250,000

The most experienced player in the side, Masami will captain Japan in their first ever World Cup finals. No one will take more pride than Ihara in leading their country into France after a gruelling qualification round.

An extremely difficult group sees Japan rated as highly doubtful to reach any further than the group stage. With the lack of quality in the side it will be immensely tough for them.

How they got there

Asia 2nd Qualifying Round - Group B

Date	Home		Away	Score
06-Sep-97	South Korea	vs.	Kazakhstan	3-0
07-Sep-97	Japan	vs.	Uzbekistan	6-3
12-Sep-97	South Korea	vs.	Uzbekistan	2-1
12-Sep-97	UAE	vs.	Kazakhstan	4-0
19-Sep-97	UAE	vs.	Japan	0-0
20-Sep-97	Kazakhstan	vs.	Uzbekistan	1-1
27-Sep-97	Uzbekistan	vs.	UAE	2-3
28-Sep-97	Japan	vs.	South Korea	1-2
04-Oct-97	South Korea	vs.	UAE	3-0
04-Oct-97	Kazakhstan	vs.	Japan	1-1
11-Oct-97	Uzbekistan	vs.	Japan	1-1
11-Oct-97	Kazakhstan	vs.	South Korea	1-1
18-Oct-97	Uzbekistan	vs.	South Korea	1-5
18-Oct-97	Kazakhstan	vs.	UAE	3-0
25-Oct-97	Uzbekistan	vs.	Kazakhstan	4-0
26-Oct-97	Japan	vs.	UAE	1-1
01-Nov-97	South Korea	vs.	Qatar	0-2
02-Nov-97	UAE	vs.	Uzbekistan	0-0
08-Nov-97	Japan	vs.	Kazakhstan	5-1
08-Nov-97	UAE	vs.	South Korea	1-3
12-Nov-97	China PR	vs.	Qatar	1-0
12-Nov-97	Qatar	vs.	Saudi Arabia	0-1

FINAL STANDINGS

Team	P	W	D	L	F	A	Pts
South Korea	8	6	1	1	19	7	19
Japan	8	3	4	1	17	9	13
UAE	8	2	3	3	9	12	9
Uzbekistan	8	1	3	4	13	18	6
Kazakhstan	8	1	3	4	7	19	6

Japan Qualify for finals by beating Iran in Play-Off

World Cup Odds

300/1

MEXICO

Carlos Hermisollo

Age	Caps	Value
33	95	£500,000

Now playing his football for Cruz Azul, Carlos has been an outstanding servant to the Mexican team. A fiery midfielder who leads the team with great passion.

Carlos has seen the rise and demise of the Mexican game and with nearly 100 caps he will be hoping that he can bow out of his international career with pride.

Group E

Saturday June 13
MEXICO V SOUTH KOREA

Saturday June 20
MEXICO V BELGIUM

Thursday June 25
MEXICO V HOLLAND

ONE TO WATCH

Jorge Campos

Age	Caps	Value
31	97	£2 million

Colourful Jorge Campos is always being touted as one of the attractions of the game - even if he is one of the most inconsistent goalkeepers around. His brightly coloured goalkeepers' jerseys are always eye-catching along with his acrobatic manoeuvres to make a save.

Not only does he spring around the Penalty area but he also fancies himself as a bit of a striker - and do not be surprised if he is called up to the attacking line if need be.

How they got there

Concacaf Final Round

Date	Home		Away	Score
02-Mar-97	Mexico	vs.	Canada	4-0
02-Mar-97	Jamaica	vs.	USA	0-0
16-Mar-97	USA	vs.	Canada	3-0
16-Mar-97	Costa Rica	vs.	Mexico	0-0
23-Mar-97	Costa Rica	vs.	Canada	3-2
06-Apr-97	Canada	vs.	El Salvador	0-0
13-Apr-97	Mexico	vs.	Jamaica	6-0
20-Apr-97	USA	vs.	Mexico	2-2
27-Apr-97	Canada	vs.	Jamaica	0-0
04-May-97	El Salvador	vs.	Costa Rica	2-1
11-May-97	Costa Rica	vs.	Jamaica	3-1
18-May-97	Jamaica	vs.	El Salvador	1-0
01-Jun-97	Canada	vs.	Costa Rica	1-0
08-Jun-97	El Salvador	vs.	Mexico	0-1
29-Jun-97	El Salvador	vs.	USA	1-1
10-Aug-97	Costa Rica	vs.	El Salvador	0-0
07-Sep-97	USA	vs.	Costa Rica	1-0
07-Sep-97	Jamaica	vs.	Canada	1-0
14-Sep-97	Jamaica	vs.	Costa Rica	1-0
14-Sep-97	El Salvador	vs.	Canada	4-1
03-Oct-97	USA	vs.	Jamaica	1-1
05-Oct-97	Mexico	vs.	El Salvador	5-0
12-Oct-97	Canada	vs.	Mexico	2-2
02-Nov-97	Mexico	vs.	USA	0-0
09-Nov-97	Canada	vs.	USA	0-3
09-Nov-97	El Salvador	vs.	Jamaica	2-2
09-Nov-97	Mexico	vs.	Costa Rica	3-3
16-Nov-97	Jamaica	vs.	Mexico	0-0
16-Nov-97	Costa Rica	vs.	Canada	3-1
16-Nov-97	USA	vs.	El Salvador	4-2

FINAL STANDINGS

Mexico	10	4	6	0	23	7	18
USA	10	4	5	1	17	8	17
Jamaica	10	3	5	2	7	12	14
Costa Rica	10	3	3	4	13	12	12
El Salvador	10	2	4	4	11	16	10
Canada	10	1	3	6	5	20	6

Mexico, USA, Jamaica, Costa Rica Qualified for finals

World Cup Odds

80/1

Salahdine Bassir

Age	Caps	Value
25	21	£4 million

10 goals in the qualifying stages saw Salahdine Bassir become one of the players that is worshipped by the fanatical Moroccan fans. Now playing for Deportivo in Spain, he has a firm ambition to become one of the greatest strikers in the world.

He is very quick and lively in and around the penalty area, making goals not too hard to come by. A prolific goalscorer, he could be brought back down to the ground when coming up against such defences as the Brazilian and Norwegian.

Group A

Wednesday June 10
MOROCCO V NORWAY

Tuesday June 16
MOROCCO V BRAZIL

Tuesday June 23
MOROCCO V SCOTLAND

How they got there

Nourredine Naybet

Age	Caps	Value
27	84	£2.5 million

The defensive pillar of the team, he is the captain and natural leader on and off the pitch. Once thought of as a liability because of his bad temperament, he has cooled down and has benefited from it.

Immensely strong he will match any attacker for power but he could be tested when it comes to his lack of pace, though often gets away with it because of the wonderful way in which he reads the game.

African Group 5

Date	Home		Away	Score
09-Nov-96	Morocco	vs.	Sierra Leone	4:0
10-Nov-96	Gabon	vs.	Ghana	1:1
11-Jan-97	Sierra Leone	vs.	Gabon	1:0
12-Jan-97	Ghana	vs.	Morocco	2:2
05-Apr-97	Sierra Leone	vs.	Ghana	1:1
06-Apr-97	Gabon	vs.	Morocco	0:4
26-Apr-97	Sierra Leone	vs.	Morocco	0:1
27-Apr-97	Ghana	vs.	Gabon	3:0
08-Jun-97	Gabon	vs.	Sierra Leone	never played
06-Jun-97	Morocco	vs.	Ghana	1:0
17-Aug-97	Morocco	vs.	Gabon	2:0
17-Aug-97	Ghana	vs.	Sierra Leone	0:2

FINAL STANDINGS

Team	P	W	D	L	F	A	Pts
Morocco	6	5	1	0	14	2	16
Sierra Leone	5	2	1	2	4	6	7
Ghana	6	1	3	2	7	7	6
Gabon	5	0	1	4	1	11	1

World Cup Odds

150/1

Aristidies Rojas

Age	Caps	Value
29	n/a	£1.5million

Delightful midfield playmaker who loves to take on defences with his exquisite skills. He is not one of the players that is always singled out, but many believe that he will really shine in France.

The abundance of midfield talent is what ultimately saw Paraguay through to the World Cup. Along with Rojas, players such as Acuna and Acre can destroy opposing teams with their skill and vision.

Group D

Friday June 12 **PARAGUAY V BULGARIA**
Friday June 19 **PARAGUAY V SPAIN**
Wednesday June 24 **PARAGUAY V NIGERIA**

PARAGUAY

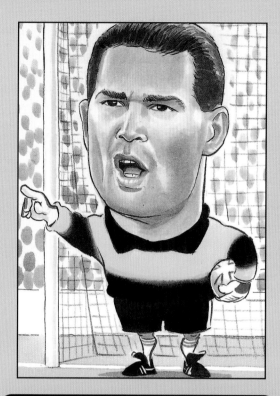

How they got there

Jose Luis Chilavert

Age	Caps	Value
32	n/a	£ 1 million

Surely one of the most extrovert players to be going to France this summer. Though he plays in a goalkeeper's position, he has a good goalscoring record and regularly comes forward to take free-kicks and penalties.

He is the captain and has proved how vital his inspiration is to the squad. Though tremendously talented, he has a rash temper which saw him serve a four-match ban during qualification. Paraguay went on to lose all four games that Chilavert could not play in.

FINAL STANDINGS

South American

24-Apr-96	Columbia	vs.	Paraguay	1:0
02-Jun-96	Uraguay	vs.	Paraguay	0:2
01-Sep-96	Argentina	vs.	Paraguay	1:1
09-Oct-96	Paraguay	vs.	Chile	2:1
10-Nov-96	Paraguay	vs.	Equador	1:0
15-Dec-96	Bolivia	vs.	Paraguay	0:0
12-Jan-97	Venezuala	vs.	Paraguay	0:2
12-Feb-97	Paraguay	vs.	Peru	2:1
02-Apr-97	Paraguay	vs.	Columbia	2:1
30-Apr-97	Paraguay	vs.	Uraguay	3:1
06-Jul-97	Paraguay	vs.	Argentina	1:2
20-Jul-97	Chile	vs.	Paraguay	2:1
20-Aug-97	Equador	vs.	Paraguay	2:1
10-Sep-97	Paraguay	vs.	Bolivia	2:1
12-Oct-97	Paraguay	vs.	Venezuala	1:0
16-Nov-97	Peru	vs.	Paraguay	1:0

SOUTH AMERICA - ROUND ROBIN QUALIFIERS

Argentina	16	8	6	2	23	13	30
Paraguay	16	9	2	5	21	14	29
Colombia	16	8	4	4	23	15	28
Chile	16	7	4	5	32	18	25

Top 4 teams qualified

World Cup Odds

80/1

SAUDI ARABIA

Fuad Amin

Age	Caps	Value
24	n/a	£2 million

The Saudi team come into this World Cup with very little chance of success, but there are players in the squad who are hoping to make a name for themselves and Fuad Amin is one of them.

An attacking midfield player who likes to run at defences he was instrumental in the qualification rounds.

Group C

Friday June 12
SAUDI ARABIA V DENMARK

Thursday June 18
SAUDI ARABIA V FRANCE

Wednesday June 24
SAUDI ARABIA V SOUTH AFRICA

SAUDI ARABIA

Fahad Al-Mehalel

Age	Caps	Value
27	n/a	£2 million

Saudi rules state that there are only a select few players who are allowed to leave the country to go and play abroad. Al-Mehalel is one who looks certain to be granted his dream of playing in Europe if he performs come June.

A talented player who is extremely versatile, he can actually play in virtually any position on the pitch.

How they got there

Asia and Qualifying Round - Group A

Date	Home		Away	Score
13-Sep-97	China PR	vs.	Iran	2-4
14-Sep-97	Saudi Arabia	vs.	Kuwait	2-1
19-Sep-97	Iran	vs.	Saudi Arabia	1-1
19-Sep-97	Qatar	vs.	Kuwait	0-2
26-Sep-97	Kuwait	vs.	Iran	1-1
26-Sep-97	Qatar	vs.	China PR	1-1
03-Oct-97	China PR	vs.	Saudi Arabia	1-0
03-Oct-97	Iran	vs.	Qatar	3-0
10-Oct-97	Kuwait	vs.	China PR	1-2
11-Oct-97	Saudi Arabia	vs.	Qatar	1-0
17-Oct-97	Iran	vs.	China PR	4-1
17-Oct-97	Kuwait	vs.	Saudi Arabia	2-1
24-Oct-97	Kuwait	vs.	Qatar	0-1
24-Oct-97	Saudi Arabia	vs.	Qatar	1-0
31-Oct-97	China PR	vs.	Qatar	2-3
31-Oct-97	Iran	vs.	Qatar	0-0
06-Nov-97	Saudi Arabia	vs.	China PR	1-1
07-Nov-97	Qatar	vs.	Iran	2-0
12-Nov-97	China PR	vs.	Qatar	1-0
12-Nov-97	Qatar	vs.	Saudi Arabia	0-1

FINAL STANDINGS

Saudi Arabia	8	4	2	2	8	6	14
Iran	8	3	3	2	13	8	12
China PR	8	3	2	3	11	14	11
Qatar	8	3	1	4	7	10	10
Kuwait	8	2	2	4	7	8	8

World Cup Odds

200/1

Lucas Radebe

Age	Caps	Value
28	33	£3 million

A very impressive Leeds United defender who recently was given the honour of captaining his country. Though played at a more preferred defensive position for his club, it is in the midfield where South Africa feel he is most effective.

He has improved his game ten-fold over the past few seasons and has matured into what many Leeds United fans believe is one of the best defenders in the English Premiership.

Group C

Friday June 12
SOUTH AFRICA V FRANCE

Thursday June 18
SOUTH AFRICA V DENMARK

Wednesday June 24
SOUTH AFRICA V SAUDI ARABIA

Phil Masinga

Age	Caps	Value
28	33	£2 million

After initially proving a useful player in the Premiership he found it hard to settle in and it is now at Bari where Phil is playing at the highest level. He is vital to the South African team - and has shown that by scoring some vital goals in the qualification rounds.

It looks as though he has formed a deadly partnership with wonderkind Benedict McCarthy which could turn a few heads this summer.

How they got there

Africa 2nd Qualifying Round - Group 3

Date	Home		Away	Score
10-Nov-96	South Africa	vs.	Zaire	1-0
10-Nov-96	Congo	vs.	Zambia	1-0
11-Jan-97	Zambia	vs.	South Africa	0-0
12-Jan-97	Zaire	vs.	Congo	1-1
06-Apr-97	Congo	vs.	South Africa	2-0
06-Apr-97	Zaire	vs.	Zambia	2-2
27-Apr-97	Zambia	vs.	Congo	3-0
27-Apr-97	Tunisia	vs.	South Africa	1-2
08-Jun-97	Congo	vs.	Zaire	1-0
08-Jun-97	South Africa	vs.	Tunisia	3-0
17-Aug-97	South Africa	vs.	Congo	1-0
17-Aug-97	Zambia	vs.	Zaire	2-0

FINAL STANDINGS

Team	P	W	D	L	F	A	Pts
South Africa	6	4	1	0	7	3	13
Congo	6	3	1	2	5	5	10
Zambia	6	2	2	4	7	6	8
Zaire	6	0	2	4	4	9	2

South Africa Qualify for finals

World Cup Odds

100/1

Sung Yung Choi

Age	Caps	Value
22	14	£2 million

A prolific goalscorer for his national team and in the domestic league. He is one of the brightest players to come out of the Far East for quite a while and is being closely watched by many top teams.

He recently performed well in the Kings Cup and there is every chance of him notching a few goals for his country in France.

Group E

Saturday June 13
SOUTH KOREA V MEXICO

Saturday June 20
SOUTH KOREA V HOLLAND

Thursday June 25
SOUTH KOREA V BELGIUM

SOUTH KOREA

How they got there

ONE TO WATCH

Seo Jung Wong

Age	Caps	Value
27	72	£500,000

A very experienced player who can play in a variety of positions but is preferred in a striker's role. Given that he is one of the oldest in the squad, it does show the youth of the South Korean team.

Players like Seo Jung Wong are going to prove vital if South Korea are going to hold their own in France, so many times they have come along to make up the numbers, could this year be any different?

Asia 2nd Qualifying Round - Group B

06-Sep-97	South Korea	vs.	Kazakhstan	3-0
07-Sep-97	Japan	vs.	Uzbekistan	6-3
12-Sep-97	South Korea	vs.	Uzbekistan	2-1
12-Sep-97	UAE	vs.	Kazakhstan	4-0
19-Sep-97	UAE	vs.	Japan	0-0
20-Sep-97	Kazakhstan	vs.	Uzbekistan	1-1
27-Sep-97	Uzbekistan	vs.	UAE	2-3
28-Sep-97	Japan	vs.	South Korea	1-2
04-Oct-97	South Korea	vs.	UAE	3-0
04-Oct-97	Kazakhstan	vs.	Japan	1-1
11-Oct-97	Uzbekistan	vs.	Japan	1-1
11-Oct-97	Kazakhstan	vs.	South Korea	1-1
18-Oct-97	Uzbekistan	vs.	South Korea	1-5
18-Oct-97	Kazakhstan	vs.	UAE	3-0
25-Oct-97	Uzbekistan	vs.	Kazakhstan	4-0
26-Oct-97	Japan	vs.	UAE	1-1
01-Nov-97	South Korea	vs.	Qatar	0-2
02-Nov-97	UAE	vs.	Uzbekistan	0-0
08-Nov-97	Japan	vs.	Kazakhstan	5-1
08-Nov-97	UAE	vs.	South Korea	1-3
12-Nov-97	China PR	vs.	Qatar	1-0
12-Nov-97	Qatar	vs.	Saudi Arabia	0-1

FINAL STANDINGS

South Korea	8	6	1	1	19	7	19
Japan	8	3	4	1	17	9	13
UAE	8	2	3	3	9	12	9
Uzbekistan	8	1	3	4	13	18	6
Kazakhstan	8	1	3	4	7	19	6

Japan Qualify for finals by beating Iran in Play-Off

World Cup Odds

150/1

TUNISIA

Adel Sellimi

Age	Caps	Value
26	52	£2 million

Tunisian footballer of the year on many occasions, Adel Sellimi finds himself out of the picture leading up to the World Cup. Undoubtedly talented but a lack of form for French club Nantes saw him dropped by the national team coach.

A move to the Spanish second division has helped resurrect his international career, but he really must try to regain the form which saw so many teams after him a few years ago. On his day a superb footballer who can play with the best.

Group G

Monday June 15
TUNISIA V ENGLAND

Monday June 22
TUNISIA V COLUMBIA

Friday June 26
TUNISIA V ROMANIA

How they got there

Chokri El Ouaer

Age	Caps	Value
31	50	£250,000

A veteran goalkeeper who, though not the most spectacular of number one's, is solid and very reliable. He is facing tough competition for his place but his experience should see him through to the starting line-up.

Tunisia are thought of as the weakest in their group but they are resolute about their chances and could make the headlines. They have many underrated players who have a chance to put one over on some of the biggest teams in the world.

Africa 2nd Qualifying Round - Group 2

Date	Home		Away	Score
06-Nov-96	Egypt	vs.	Namibia	7-1
10-Nov-96	Liberia	vs.	Tunisia	0-1
11-Jan-97	Namibia	vs.	Liberia	0-0
12-Jan-97	Tunisia	vs.	Egypt	1-0
06-Apr-97	Liberia	vs.	Egypt	1-0
06-Apr-97	Namibia	vs.	Tunisia	1-2
26-Apr-97	Namibia	vs.	Egypt	2-3
27-Apr-97	Tunisia	vs.	Liberia	2-0
08-Jun-97	Liberia	vs.	Namibia	1-2
08-Jun-97	Egypt	vs.	Tunisia	0-0
17-Aug-97	Egypt	vs.	Liberia	5-0
17-Aug-97	Tunisia	vs.	Namibia	4-0

FINAL STANDINGS

Team	P	W	D	L	F	A	Pts
Tunisia	6	5	1	0	10	1	16
Egypt	6	3	1	2	15	5	10
Liberia	6	1	1	4	2	10	4
Namibia	6	1	1	4	6	17	4

Tunisia Qualify for finals

World Cup Odds

300/1

Eric Wynalda

Age	Caps	Value
28	90	£3 million

The slow rise of American 'soccer' since the World Cup four years ago has not seen a dramatic rise in top American players, but Eric Wynalda has continued to prosper and show the world he can play with the big boys.

A skilful striker who loves to tantalise defenders with his speed and trickery, he is the main weapon the USA have in their armoury. He will continue to look to further his career after France and a move to the Premiership is definitely a consideration.

Group F

Monday June 15
USA V GERMANY

Sunday June 21
USA V IRAN

Thursday June 25
USA V YUGOSLAVIA

ONE TO WATCH

John Harkes

Age	Caps	Value
30	83	£1 million

After stints at several clubs in the
Premiership, especially at Sheffield
Wednesday, he came back to the States
to attract fans to Major League Soccer,
the American version of the English
Premiership. Though the standard does
not even come close to comparison, John
is somewhat of an idol and is now
captain of the national side.

He likes to play in midfield, but can play
in the defence, he is hard in the tackle
and a decent tackler of the ball.

How they got there

Concaraf qualifying group

Date	Home		Away	Score
02-Mar-97	Mexico	vs.	Canada	4-0
02-Mar-97	Jamaica	vs.	USA	0-0
16-Mar-97	USA	vs.	Canada	3-0
16-Mar-97	Costa Rica	vs.	Mexico	0-0
23-Mar-97	Costa Rica	vs.	Canada	3-2
23-Mar-97	Costa Rica	vs.	USA	3-2
06-Apr-97	Canada	vs.	El Salvador	0-0
13-Apr-97	Mexico	vs.	Jamaica	6-0
20-Apr-97	USA	vs.	Mexico	2-2
27-Apr-97	Canada	vs.	Jamaica	0-0
04-May-97	El Salvador	vs.	Costa Rica	2-1
11-May-97	Costa Rica	vs.	Jamaica	3-1
18-May-97	Jamaica	vs.	El Salvador	1-0
01-Jun-97	Canada	vs.	Costa Rica	1-0
08-Jun-97	El Salvador	vs.	Mexico	0-1
29-Jun-97	El Salvador	vs.	USA	1-1
10-Aug-97	Costa Rica	vs.	El Salvador	0-0
07-Sep-97	USA	vs.	Costa Rica	1-0
07-Sep-97	Jamaica	vs.	Canada	1-0
14-Sep-97	Jamaica	vs.	Costa Rica	1-0
14-Sep-97	El Salvador	vs.	Canada	4-1
03-Oct-97	USA	vs.	Jamaica	1-1
05-Oct-97	Mexico	vs.	El Salvador	5-0
12-Oct-97	Canada	vs.	Mexico	2-2
02-Nov-97	Mexico	vs.	USA	0-0
09-Nov-97	Canada	vs.	USA	0-3
09-Nov-97	El Salvador	vs.	Jamaica	2-2
09-Nov-97	Mexico	vs.	Costa Rica	3-3
16-Nov-97	Jamaica	vs.	Mexico	0-0
16-Nov-97	Costa Rica	vs.	Canada	3-1
16-Nov-97	USA	vs.	El Salvador	4-2

FINAL STANDINGS

Mexico	10	4	6	0	23	7	18
USA	10	4	5	1	17	8	17
Jamaica	10	3	5	2	7	12	14
Costa Rica	10	3	3	4	13	12	12
El Salvador	10	2	4	4	11	16	10
Canada	10	1	3	6	5	20	6

Mexico,USA, Jamaica,Costa Rica Qualified for finals

World Cup Odds

150/1

GROUP A
1. BRAZIL
2. SCOTLAND
3. MOROCCO
4. NORWAY

GROUP B
1. ITALY
2. CHILE
3. CAMEROON
4. AUSTRIA

GROUP C
1. FRANCE
2. SOUTH AFRICA
3. SAUDI ARABIA
4. DENMARK

GROUP D
1. SPAIN
2. NIGERIA
3. PARAGUAY
4. BULGARIA

GROUP E
1. HOLLAND
2. BELGIUM
3. SOUTH KOREA
4. MEXICO

GROUP F
1. GERMANY
2. USA
3. YUGOSLAVIA
4. IRAN

GROUP G
1. ROMANIA
2. COLUMBIA
3. ENGLAND
4. TUNISIA

GROUP H
1. ARGENTINA
2. JAPAN
3. JAMAICA
4. CROATIA

Winner Group A ....
Winner Group B ....

Sat June 27 Paris (8pm)

Winner Group C ....
Winner Group D ....

Sun June 28 Paris Saint Denis (8pm)

Winner Group E ....
Winner Group F ....

Mon June 29 Toulouse (8pm)

Winner Group G ....
Winner Group H ....

Tue June 30 St Etienne (8pm)

Winner Group A ....
Winner Group B ....

Sat June 30 Marseille (3.30pm)

Winner Group C ....
Winner Group D ....

Sun June 28 Lens (3.30pm)

Winner Group E ....
Winner Group F ....

Mon June 29 Montpellier (3.30pm)

Winner Group G ....
Winer Group H ....

Tue June 30 Bordeux (3.30pm)

TOURNAMENT

Fri July 3 Nantes (8pm)

Tue July 7 Marseille (8pm)

Sat July 4 Marseille (3.30pm)

Sun July 12 Paris Saint Denis (8pm)

Fri July 3 Paris Saint Denis (3.30pm)

Wed July 8 Paris Saint Denis (8pm)

Sat July 4 Lyon (8pm)

3rd & 4th place play off for semi final losers

Sat July 11 Paris (8pm)

Paolo Maldini
Italy

David Beckham
England

Peter Schmeichel
Denmark

Matthias Sammer
Germany

Lillian Thuram
France

Franck De Boer
Holland

DREAM TEAM

Zinedine Zidane
France

Marcelo Salas
Chile

Ronaldo
Brazil

Denilson
Brazil

Raul
Spain

LIMITED EDITION PROMATCH FRAMED MEDALLIONS SETS

Each medallion is set in a laminated card, individually named and mounted in a Plexiglass 14" x 9" frame.

OUT NOW!

England World Cup '98 Frame	*World Cup '98 Frame*	*Scotland World Cup '98 Frame*
£14.95 Cat no WCFM3	**£17.95 Cat no WCFM1**	**£12.95 Cat no WCFM2**
Frame Colour -White	**Frame Colour -Red or black (please state preference)**	**Frame Colour -Blue**

ENGLAND WORLD CUP '98 MEDALLIONS

DAVID SEAMAN	NICKY BUTT
TIM FLOWERS	DAVID BECKHAM
IAN WALKER	STEVE MCMANAMAN
GRAEME LE SAUX	ROBBIE FOWLER
TONY ADAMS	PAUL SCHOLES
GARY NEVILLE	ROBERT LEE
GARETH SOUTHGATE	LES FERDINAND
DAVID BATTY	ALAN SHEARER
STUART PEARCE	TEDDY SHERINGHAM
PHIL NEVILLE	IAN WRIGHT
PAUL INCE	RIO FERDINAND
PAUL GASCOIGNE	ANDY HINCHCLIFF
GLENN HODDLE	IAN WRIGHT
SOL CAMPBELL	NIGEL MARTYN
JAMIE REDKNAPP	

WORLD CUP '98 SUPERSTARS MEDALLIONS

ALAN SHEARER	MIHAJLOVIC	ALI DAEL
RONALDO	DAN PETRESCU	DEON BURTON
KEVIN GALLAGHER	CELESTINE BABAYARO	KAZUYOSHI MIURE
MATHIAS SAMMER		CARLOS HERMOSILLO
ZINEDINE ZIDANE	HRISTO STOICHKOV	SIAHEDDINE BASSIR
GIANFRANCO ZOLA	OLE-GUNNAR SOLSKJAER	
RAUL		ARISTIDES ROJAS
DENNIS BERGKAMP	TONY POLSTER	FUAD AMIN
GABRIEL BASTISTUTA	GILLES DE BILDE	LUCAS RADEBE
BRIAN LAUDRUP	JAQUES SONGO'O	SUNG-YONG CHOI
SLAVEN BILIC	MARCELO SALAS	ADEL SELLIMI
SINISA	FAUSTINO ASPRILLA	ERIC WYNALDA

SCOTLAND WORLD CUP '98 MEDALLIONS

ANDY GORAM	DAVID HOPKIN
SCOTT BOOTH	DARREN JACKSON
TOMMY BOYD	MATT ELLIOTT
CRAIG BURLEY	JIM LEIGHTON
COLIN CAULDERWOOD	GARY MCALLISTER
JOHN COLLINS	STUART MCCALL
CRISTIAN DAILY	BILLY MCKINLAY
GORDON DURIE	TOSH MCKINLAY
DUNCAN FERGUSON	JACKIE MCNAMARA
CRAIG BROWN	NEIL SULLIVAN
KEVIN GALLAGHER	
COLIN HENDRY	

For further details please call (0181) 938 4613 or fax (0181) 938 4615